Brylcreem Summer

BRYLCREEM SUMMER

The 1947 Cricket Season

ERIC MIDWINTER

THE KINGSWOOD PRESS

First published in Great Britain in 1991
by The Kingswood Press
an imprint of Methuen London
Michelin House, 81 Fulham Road, London SW3 6RB

A CIP catalogue record for this book
is available from the British Library

ISBN 0 413 64380 8

Typeset by Deltatype Ltd, Ellesmere Port
Printed in Great Britain
by Clays Ltd, St. Ives plc

Contents

Acknowledgements

The photographs of Athol Rowan at Worcester, Tufty Mann at Cambridge, Dudley Nourse batting against MCC and England, Alan Melville, Alan Melville and Dennis Dyer, Ken Cranston and the Middlesex team are reproduced by kind permission of Sport & General. All the other photographs are reproduced by kind permission of the Hulton Picture Company.

At the Kingswood Press, it is only right that I should thank Tony Pocock and Neil Tunnicliffe for their expert help and sympathetic support in preparing the book for press.

London
March 1991

Eric Midwinter

Introduction

My own schoolboy cricketing summer of 1947 was the most ragged season in a totally nondescript acquaintance with the playing side of the game, but I have two memories of proper cricket that more than compensate for the personal humiliations. My father, of a sudden, took a friend and I to Old Trafford, just five minutes away on the train, for the second day of the Sussex match. We watched the later Sussex batting removed, giving a Lancashire lead of 3 runs. Cyril Washbrook then hit the first Sussex delivery for 6, and that precipitated a glorious cavalcade of runs from 'Washy' and his lugubrious partner, Winston Place. They scored 350 in three hours and fifty minutes, Washbrook 204 and Place 134 – and not forgetting that Sussex bowled 80 overs in that time, more than 20 an hour. It was 18 short of the Lancashire first-wicket record, which had stood since 1903, but remains the county's highest unbroken partnership.

Later that year the family stayed with an elderly relative near Tunbridge Wells, and that marked our first-ever visit to London. My father, always an astute student of fixture-lists, engineered the holiday to coincide with Lancashire playing at Lord's, so that, wonderfully, my first trip to Mecca was to watch my own heroes. Again, we arrived – 'just for an hour' said father to unbelieving mother – on the second day, Lancashire having scored 352 on the opening day. Compton was bowled cheaply round his legs by Ikin, our tiny northern cries breaking the stunned hush of thousands, and Middlesex were all out for 134, the left-hander Eric Price and John Ikin taking the wickets. One well-remembered cameo is of Bill Edrich, boldly picking up the gauntlet of, in effect, leg-spin from both ends, advancing and driving firmly into and past that handsome and traditional arc of off-side fielders. Eventually, after scoring a fighting 55, he succumbed, driving uppishly to be caught by Alan Wharton off Ikin's leg-spin. Lancashire consolidated with 153 more runs, setting a target of 372. Although much of the limelight was upon Denis Compton, who, wonky knee and all, equalled Hobbs's record of sixteen centuries in a season, Lancashire whittled out their illustrious opponents, and won by 64 runs. That was extremely satisfying, at least for some of the 60,000 people who watched through those three warm late-summer days.

This study of 1947 owes something to such memories, for nostalgia is part of the lure of cricket. It owes more, indeed a tremendous debt, to John Arlott's mellow reverie, *Vintage Summer: 1947*, published in 1967. His evocation of that summer, and his deft descriptions of the play and the players, is an acknowledged classic. A battered 1948 *Wisden* has also, inevitably, been well-thumbed. Apart from a detailed review of the 1947 season, the attempt has been made to analyse the immediate post-war seasons, examining how the euphoria of a summer like 1947 would soon be seen as a flash in the pan, and trying to relate these events to the social background of post-war Britain against which they took place. Although a discrete study, it might, in part, be read as a sequel to my *The Lost Seasons: Cricket in Wartime; 1939–1945.*

But the summer of 1947 is the unrivalled hero. It *was* a Brylcreem summer. It had that same sparkle and sheen, and that heady hint of romantic promise. With Denis Compton the splendid advocate of the pleasures of 1947 and thereafter forever to be associated with that famous hair-cream, there came a further connotation. There was a bravura touch of RAF swagger about 1947, when the flying men were known as Brylcreem Boys. Moreover, there is something about hair-cream that smoothly masks a more hurtful truth – and the cricket of 1947 certainly did that, raising all kinds of optimistic hopes for the future. Thus the summer of 1947 may be cast as metaphor for post-war society, with its ideal aspirations eventually dashed in humdrum, sometimes unpleasant, circumstance. Yet it was truly a glorious cricket season. Nobody who was, as cricketers say, there or thereabouts, ever forgets 1947.

PART ONE

Prelude

1

The Legacy of War

'There'll be bluebirds', crooned Vera Lynn, 'over the white cliffs of Dover, tomorrow, just you wait and see'. Cricket's equivalent of that avian revisitation occurred at 11.30 on Saturday 4 May 1946, when a first-class programme began after the longest hiatus since the concept of first-class cricket had been acknowledged.

The 1946 season closely resembled the 1939 season. Of course there were changes, consequent on the tragic deaths of men like Maurice Turnbull, Ken Farnes and Hedley Verity, each in his own right irreplaceable. There were also others who, by eager choice or less willingly, played little or no first-class cricket again, and, with the qualification rules relaxed, there was also some slight movement of players between counties.

There were virtuous and wholesome reasons for this conservationist mood: the doctrine of 'resettlement' on demobilisation, requested by government and demanded by the public, required that service personnel should return if they wished to their previous employ, and county cricket clubs wholeheartedly fell in with this patriotic notion. Next, in that crowds were anxious to catch a last glimpse of these old pre-war-horses, this was a bonus, for many paraded their talents for a final season or two in this manner. On the negative side, it was these very stars, whom the public flocked to see, who had seized the limited opportunities of big-time cricket during the war. With unkempt grounds and inadequate coaching, it was the younger generation who suffered the most, and this lack of a chance of an apprenticeship was to prove a most taxing factor in England's attempt at a cricketing recovery.

But the chief reason why the 1946 season so closely resembled 1939 concerned the impact of Vera Lynn's prophecy about the bluebirds' return. It is quite apparent, in any study of the thinking and writing about the Second World War, that there were two distinctive, even contradictory, sets of post-war aims. Sometimes the threads were tangled, either nationally or individually, but their colouring always remained distinct. On the one side there were those, disgusted by the failure to honour the sacrifice of the first war with a decent, civilised society, who vowed that post-1945 a new future must and should be planned and freshly resolved. On the other side, there were those who had found comfort and solace in the 1920s and 1930s, and who fought the war to restore that precious life-style. These were the ones who scanned the skies for the homecoming of the bluebird.

The cricketing authorities almost entirely belonged to that second school of thought. The static, introverted, deadening years between the wars had left them untouched. The harsh winds of the depression, for instance, had blown less chillingly for some people and in some areas, and the establishment wished for nothing more than the comfortable and comforting familiarities. There can be little doubt now that they made a grave strategic mistake. By insisting that first-class cricket should not be subjected to any change whatsoever they effectively guaranteed that, when cricket was in real crisis in the 1950s and early 1960s, the measures forced upon it were piecemeal and the result of panic, so much so that cricket's survival has been uneasy and partial. First-class cricket was in the position of the sick patient who, by postponing his visit to the doctor until almost too late, finds himself subject to heroic and emergency surgery with a poor prognosis for eventual full recovery.

Some might think this an abrasive judgement, based on the smug assessment of hindsight, but this is not the case. The testimony of cricket in the war was there for consideration, but the wrong lessons were learned, while throughout the war years a debate about the future of cricket was briskly maintained but with all the progressive suggestions being totally ignored.

Although, by some accounts, cricket had a good war, it did not use unusual opportunities to build and develop. Football, pubs, theatre, ballet, serious music, cinema, radio and ballroom dancing form a mixed bag of leisure activities which made considerable headway during the war, in terms of popular support as well as in styles and approaches. From the leisure viewpoint, it was a most curious war. It brought full employment and high wages alongside rationing and transport and other restrictions. Britain was also much more of an island fortress than in the First World War, either preparing to resist invasion from or to carry invasion to the Continent. Expenditure on leisure rose 120 per cent, and certainly cricket gained from this. But there was no attempt to maintain a rudimentary county or allied competition, although several counties – notably Nottinghamshire – struggled along, and a regional contest had been mooted. Worst of all, although somewhat shortsighted endeavours were made to sustain public school cricket, children at large, taking into account the trials of evacuation and the loss of many young sports teachers to the colours, were granted little priority.

What there was was very good indeed. There was cricket, especially at Lord's but also elsewhere, of high competence and much excitement. Two nomadic factions, the London Counties XI and the British Empire XI, took on some of the mantle of the Players and Gentlemen respectively, and revived dim memories of the old Victorian Exhibition XIs as they brought excellent cricket to many locations. With teams of county and Test standard selected around the armed forces and civil defence groupings, and with a prominent dash of colour and panache provided by overseas servicemen, there were some great games. And they attracted great crowds. In 1943 over 230,000 people watched the Lord's schedule of sixteen major one-day games and a number of lesser matches – as compared to 330,000 who watched a full programme of three-day county and other matches in 1939. The attendance of some 90,000 at the fourth Victory Test at Lord's in 1945 remains a ground record. Nottinghamshire invariably attracted bigger crowds for their list of nine or ten fixtures than for their 1939 county programme. In 1944 and 1945 they averaged 2,300 a day, while in 1939 they only twice had gates of over 2,000.

But the portents were misread. Sir Home Gordon, the celebrated cricket historian and pundit, noted that 'the public went to see stars not results' and observed that 'one wartime development is that spectators have become thrilled over close finishes'. This was so true, but it was not heeded. It was urged that 'the game will be more popular than ever' after the war and would emerge 'stronger than subject to increased public ownership and control (as it had been in the war); a move towards the decolonisation of Empire; a shift towards improved housing, much of it in the municipal sector; above all, a massive construct of welfare supports, majoring in the National Health Service and on 'cradle to grave' national insurance – these were the great changes of the post-1945 period and, in overall character, they came to be accepted for some thirty-five years by the political establishment. In other fields – aviation, broadcasting, medicine – war was also the catalyst for vigorous improvement. But not so cricket.

Yet the cricket authorities, caught up in the heady breeze, did flirt with reconstruction. What is surprising and frustrating is that, having bothered to analyse problems and muse over solutions, they ultimately opted for no change. As early as 1941, *The Cricketer Annual* placed its proposals for cricket among 'the plans for the betterment of the world', even as the Luftwaffe pounded away nightly. In 1942 both *Wisden* and *The Cricketer* were happy to contemplate two-day county matches, but Sir Pelham Warner and Sir Stanley Jackson spoke of 'the danger of tinkering with the game'. The Findlay Commission of 1937 had decided against the two-day match but had, on the other hand, suggested a reduced number of first-class counties and more representative games. There was also support for 'a welcome total deletion of all distinction' between amateurs and professionals. However, Pelham Warner stoutly pronounced that 'I can see nothing wrong with modern cricket'.

That was that. In July 1943 the Advisory County Cricket Committee plumped emphatically for three-day play in all games, and requested MCC to appoint a Select Committee to examine the other questions about the future of the first-class game. This panel published its report in March 1944. The committee consisted of an assemblage of well-respected cricketing notables, almost all of whom, despite or because of their experience, were backward-looking. In a phrase, there was no reconstruction. Probably no other institution underwent such an investigation in the climate of the war and emerged unscathed and untainted by alteration.

There was an airy-fairy appeal for a more 'dynamic attitude' and a hollow call to 'aim for victory from the first ball', while, on the credit side, there was a rationalisation of fixtures, with every county played in a pattern of ten double fixtures, home and away, and six single ones. All else was negative. There was to be no 'compulsory elimination' or amalgamation of counties; no Central Fund or pooling of receipts; no eight-ball overs; no Sunday cricket; no time-limit cricket, by clock, overs or scoring rate; and no change from the 1939 system of twelve points for a win and the often stultifying four points for first innings lead. An emergency regional scheme was erected, should the war end suddenly and cricket have to recommence briskly, possibly amid chaotic transport problems: it is important to recall that a regional scheme was, in fact, contemplated.

The report was 'accepted without amendment' by the Advisory Committee in October 1944, and the only outstanding issue of any note was cup cricket. The Select Committee, predictably, continued to believe that anything other than three-day cricket would be damaging. This immediately made a knockout contest impractical, because of the likelihood of stoppages for rain and drawn games of the traditional kind. There were further debates, but in November 1946 the Advisory County Cricket Committee 'decided to defer further consideration' and the matter was indefinitely shelved.

It is significant that, along with many others, the cricketing establishment did valiantly approach the question of reconstruction, but, at the brink, they retreated. So absolute was the withdrawal that the cynic might begin to suspect that the exercise was cosmetic. That is unlikely. It seems that it was more a case of men feeling a duty to look for change but unable in their bones to believe in its necessity.

Sir Pelham Warner was certainly the key figure. He had evolved through the cricketing hierarchy and cricket was his life and his creed. He had done every job and held every post, and now, in his mid-60s, he was cricket's elder statesman. He kept the lamp of cricket shining throughout the war, conscious of the need for morale to be maintained and for war charities to be benefited. He was also aware of the propaganda value of cricket's ability to survive. Perhaps he exaggerated this aspect, believing cricket to be rather more important than it actually was (certainly in terms of the German mentality: a fortnight after D-Day 70,000 watched the football league play-off in Berlin between Hamburg and Dresdener

DC: that really was a refusal to be, in the Second World War cliché, 'down-hearted').

Pelham Warner held cricket in awe. He had no conception of its intrinsic ordinariness as a game. This bred a deep conservatism, so that, with the utmost dedication, he toiled to keep cricket going – and to keep it going in exactly the same direction. It was a defensive mentality, expressed in a desire to save cricket and render it free again after the war without damage. He treated cricket as many treated great treasures and valuables, including some belonging to MCC; that is, they were hidden or buried in a secure place until the danger passed, when they were then retrieved, as good as ever. Where other fields boasted and, it must be remembered, encouraged social innovators in and just after the war – one thinks of William Beveridge, Nye Bevan and Ernie Bevin, Basil Dean in the world of theatre, inventors like Frank Whittle, Bernard Montgomery – cricket was led and represented by a man set in his ways and in his ideas. Truth to tell, this was surely an accurate form of representation for the cricketing establishment, and thus Pelham Warner must be judged as holder of the old position rather than inventor of the new fashion.

The text for this sermon in retrenchment was a quote from *The Times* in 1941, to the effect that wartime cricket was 'first-class fun but not first-class cricket'. This was, it should be recalled, that brand of one-day cricket without resource to bowling, fielding or other restrictions and which was reliant on adroit captaincy, positive attack alike by batsmen and bowlers, and deft declarations, after the manner familiar to all club and school cricket. In that sense there was nothing extraordinary about it: as batting had improved, over the decades, the two-innings formula had been widely abandoned except in county (or its overseas equivalent) and international cricket, simply because four innings were no longer a practical possibility in a day.

Thus, whereas the nation chose wholesale reform in some of its dealings, cricket took the conservationist view and stayed with the conventional format. The chance to update the system was missed. While several alternatives might have been chosen, one might, as an example, consider this amalgam drawn from proposals seriously advanced during the 'reconstruction' debate. There might have been an amalgamation of the feebler counties, or their subsuming into the Minor Counties, as a prerequisite for constructing a first division of eight or ten first-class counties, with relegation to and promotion from a second division of weaker senior and stronger junior counties. This might have led to a pattern of two-day second-division and three-day first-division games, plus a select cluster of four-day representative matches, some based on regional XIs, all preparatory steps towards the five-day Test matches. This would have offered a more open-ended structure for cricketers to make their way smoothly forward in the game, without having to risk everything in the 'all or nothing' lottery of the tightly-cabined first-class ambit.

Moreover, it might have been possible to break the county monopoly of English first-class cricket with other groupings, a device the wartime experience had shown to be feasible. Examples of this might have been the combined universities, one or more representative league sides, an overseas XI, and, while national service lasted, a Combined Services team. There should have been an end to the amateur and professional dichotomy, and finally a one-day competition should have been introduced, using Sunday at least for the earlier rounds, and based on the tenets of the Gillette/NatWest tournament. Such a programme, introduced in 1946 or over the next two or three seasons, could have been the saviour of English cricket.

As it was, the county teams of 1939 reconstituted themselves as the Dads' Armies of 1946, and the season was under way without a qualm or a quiver, just as if a huge and dislocating war had never occurred. For reasons well intentioned, as well as with deplorable myopia, the cricketing authorities chose to pretend that nothing really had happened, so that the cricket supporter, reappearing at Canterbury or Worcester in 1946 with amnesia perhaps having robbed him of any memory of the recent hostilities, might have been forgiven for presuming it was the summer of 1939.

It is true that over a hundred players made their county debuts in 1946, but the great majority of them played only a game or two, and were never to be heard of again. The wholesale way in which they were discarded underlines the point that the most deleterious effect of the war on cricket was its lack of a nursery facility.

As if to endorse cricket's attachment to retrenchment, Yorkshire were top of the table, just as they had been in 1937, 1938 and 1939. They moved to the top of the table in August, and ran out fairly comfortable leaders, with sixteen wins, only one loss and 216 points. Their team was very similar to that of the 1930s. Herbert Sutcliffe and Arthur Wood, the wicket-keeper, retired, but the rest remained, familiar names, such as Len Hutton, Bill Bowes, Maurice Leyland, Wilf Barber, P. A. Gibb, E. P. Robinson, and Cyril Turner. A. B. Sellers was once more captain, with Norman Yardley his loyal adjutant. The main change was the replacement of Hedley Verity by Arthur Booth who wryly was older than Verity, celebrating his forty-third birthday in 1946. He returned from exile with Northumberland, and, in helpful conditions, took 111 wickets, headed the first-class averages, and, with fertile assistance from the off-spinner, Robinson, ensured that Yorkshire retained the Championship. It is interesting that Yorkshire turned to older age rather than fledgling youth for succour, but as Sellers, bitterly bemoaning the inadequacies of primary techniques among the younger hopefuls, was the first to press, experience was never an instantly acquired commodity.

Middlesex fought hard, their formidable batting – Brown, Robertson, Edrich and Compton, all of pre-war vintage – heralding the glories of 1947. Like Yorkshire, they won sixteen times, but they lost five games and could not quite close the gap, finishing with 204 points. The bowling of Jim Sims and Laurie Gray and the amateur zeal of R. W. V. Robins and F. G. Mann added to the nostalgia, and there was more to come. C. R. N. Maxwell was tried as wicket-keeper and found wanting, and so Fred Price, aged 44, was hauled from retirement, demonstrating, as Booth had done, that reserves were mainly to be found among the veterans.

At one point it seemed that Lancashire might be the most likely Championship winners. They won twelve of their first fifteen fixtures in the steadiest of fashions, and in mid-July were deemed favourites. Thereafter they slipped away and managed only three more victories, ending in third place with 200 points. Their lack of cohesion may have weakened them as the summer wore on, for, of the senior counties, they witnessed the most movement of players. Eddie Paynter and the wicket-keeper, Bill Farrimond, retired to the leagues; Norman Oldfield and A. E. Nutter secured contracts with Northamptonshire; two potential captains in W. H. L. Lister and T. A. Higson Jr were not available; and the well-groomed all-rounder, Jack Iddon, was killed in a car accident. In the hard-headed fashion of the time, ready-trained recruits were sought in two of Bill Edrich's brothers, Geoffrey and Eric, in B. P. King of Worcestershire, and in the Lancashire-born Glamorgan wicket-keeper, T. L. Brierley. However, Washbrook, Place, Pollard, Phillipson and Roberts remained to give a familiar look to the red rose.

Somerset enjoyed their best season since the extension of the Championship. They were fourth and won twelve games, probably their best-ever performance, although they had been third in 1892 when the county table was smaller. For a club which had experienced much chopping and changing of personnel, the sight of a veteran crew taking the field was remarkable. Gimblett, Frank Lee, Bertie Buse, Wellard, Longrigg, Luckes, Andrews and Hazell were these mainstays.

Gloucestershire also won twelve matches, but Somerset just edged them into the fifth spot. A strong combine before the war, they once more appeared well-equipped, and indeed fielded much the same team. Hammond scored heavily in 1946, and there were other famous names surrounding him, such as Charlie Barnett and Tom Goddard. They certainly hinted at what they might accomplish in 1947. Other old-timers included George Emmett, Jack Crapp, W. L. Neale, B. O. Allen, C. J. Scott, G. E. Lambert and A. E. Wilson. It was undoubtedly one of the most settled sides in the competition.

It was Glamorgan's best-ever season, despite the mournful wartime death of Maurice Turnbull. They were sixth with ten wins, and they very much benefited from rostering almost the same team as in 1939. Led by J. C. Clay, the XI normally included Dyson, Emrys Davies, Wilf Wooller, E. C. Jones, A. D. G. Matthews, and P. F. Judge from the pre-war days.

Kent and Essex maintained something like their pre-war placements, the former slipping from fifth to seventh, the latter from fourth to eighth. Although Kent had suffered more harshly than any county through the misfortunes of war – the deaths, for instance, of F. G. H. Chalk, C. P. Hamilton and G. B. Legge – a strong pre-war squad still survived. These included the famous names of Les Ames,

B. H. Valentine, Arthur Fagg, L. J. Todd, Doug Wright, T. W. Spencer, N. W. Harding, and the new star, Godfrey Evans. Essex, never at that time the most regular in terms of personnel, seemed a stranger sounding team on resumption. M. S. Nichols and Jack O'Connor had left but there still remained from the 1930s such names as Peter and Ray Smith, F. H. Vigar, T. H. Wade, Tom Pearce, and R. M. Taylor.

Worcestershire were ninth (they had been seventh in 1939) and thus maintained steady progress, assisted by stalwarts such as Edwin Cooper, Dick Howorth, Roly Jenkins, Reg Perks, A. F. T. White, P. F. Jackson, J. S. Buller, Hugo Yarnold and H. H. T. Gibbons. It was tantamount to a ready-made eleven. There were goodish displays from Hampshire, who moved from a lowly fifteenth in 1939 to tenth in 1946, although they contrived to lose fifteen of their twenty-six fixtures. They inherited practically a full side from the last years of peace: among them were Neil McCorkell, John Arnold, Jim Bailey, G. E. M. Heath, Gerry Hill, Lofty Herman, Arthur Holt and T. A. Dean. Even more to be applauded was the upward gallop of Leicestershire, from bottom, with just a single victory, to eleventh, with seven wins. They fielded such veteran campaigners as L. G. Berry, Maurice Tompkin, F. T. Prentice, Jim Sperry, V. E. Jackson and George Dawkes.

Surrey disappointed. They were twelfth, having been eighth in 1939, and they had access to a group of very experienced players. These were R. J. Gregory, Laurie Fishlock, J. F. Parker, H. S. Squires, Alf Gover, T. H. Barling, E. A. Watts, G. S. Mobey, Bernard Constable and, of course, the rising talents of the Bedser twins. Nottinghamshire, thirteenth rather than twelfth, and Warwickshire, down from eleventh to fourteenth, were much of a muchness. W. W. Keeton, G. F. H. Heane, Joe Hardstaff Jr, C. B. Harris, H. J. Butler, Arthur Jepson, Bill Voce and F. G. Woodhead had returned more or less unscathed from the war to take up their peaceful pursuits at Trent Bridge. Warwickshire, who lost fourteen matches in 1946, had a slimmer list. Bob Wyatt, Tom Dollery, Eric Hollies, Peter Cranmer and J. S. Ord were about the only players to reappear at Edgbaston after the war.

After their sturdy performances of the 1930s, Derbyshire drooped sadly, and ended in fifteenth place. Leading players, such as George

Pope and Tommy Mitchell, opted for the relative ease and calm of league cricket, but this still left a handful of very respectable county players. They included Denis Smith, A. F. Townsend, A. E. Alderman, T. S. Worthington, A. E. G. Rhodes, Harry Elliott and Bill Copson. It was a poor re-start for the Peak county. Predictably, Northamptonshire were sixteenth, just as they had been 1939. They won but twice, as opposed to once in 1939. Their promising captain, R. P. Nelson, had been killed in the war, and several of what had always been a rather tenuous combine had disappeared. Dennis Brookes, J. E. Timms, H. W. Greenwood, P. C. Davis and R. J. Partridge returned to pick up the pieces.

Finally, Sussex had a disastrous season, and finished bottom. They won four and lost eleven times, and whereas they had been tenth in 1939 they now collected only 60 points and were last for the first time since 1896. This was despite the fact that they re-mustered the Langridge brothers, George Cox, H. W. Parks, J. H. Cornford, S. C. Griffith and J. K. Nye.

Thus did the clans gather once more and, along with them, the Indian tourists. The Imperial Cricket Conference had met in January 1946 to plan a seven-year programme of international tours, which the ever-cautious MCC found much too ambitious. MCC compromised in agreeing not necessarily to send their first-choice team to what were then regarded as junior members of the group. These were West Indies, New Zealand and India, but it was not a stance which would endure for long.

The 1946 Indian tourists represented fashions old and new. They were the third All-India party and the last to visit England before partition in 1947 and the subsequent formation of Pakistan with its own Test team. They were also the first national tourists to travel by air. That would become commonplace in a decade or two, for jet flight became as indispensible to the busy pattern of international cricket as the railways had been to the regular arrangement of county cricket in the 19th century.

With the likes of Hardstaff, Simpson and Compton to enliven the scene, cricket in India had continued in reasonable fashion during the war. The Ranji Trophy had been played for, and lots of other matches, including a tour of Ceylon, had been enjoyed in relatively placid surroundings – indeed, Reg Simpson made his first-class debut for Sind. So the Indians were well-prepared for their trip.

They were led by the Nawab of Pataudi Sr, fondly remembered for the sleek fluency of his batting, especially for Oxford University. He was no longer in the best of health and suffered some injury as well and so, carrying the burden of leadership amid the problems set by war-torn Britain, he had less personal success than his reputation warranted. They had an exceptional opening batsman in V. M. Merchant. Of massive patience, of high technical acumen and of some delicacy of touch, he was without doubt one of the leading batsmen of his day, and stands second only to Bradman in the world career table with an average of 71. His colleague, V. S. Hazare, is only a little way behind at sixth, with an average of 58 – so the Indian batting was in capable hands. Hazare was also a useful bowler, while there were two other capable all-rounders in Lala Amarnath, a medium-paced bowler, and Vinoo Mankad, then regarded as the world's leading left-hand spin bowler. Mushtaq Ali was another force to be reckoned with, usually opening the innings with Merchant.

The batting generally was sound, exemplified by the fact that they broke the English last-wicket record when, against Surrey at the Oval within a few days of the tour beginning, Sarwate and Banerjee both completed centuries in their partnership of 249.

The team acquitted themselves well enough but, Mankad apart, their bowling was never as capable as their batting and their eager fielding. On a doubtful Lord's wicket in the first Test, India were cheaply dismissed twice and, although Mankad frightened England with some early bowling successes, an entrancing double century from Joe Hardstaff paved the path to a 10-wicket victory. At Old Trafford, England were asked to bat on a soft wicket following delays because of rain. Compton and Hutton did well, and then, after a solid start, Bedser, who had bowled keenly at Lord's, joined with Dick Pollard to skittle the Indians. Compton saved England's second attempt from meagreness, but in spite of Alec Bedser's labours the Indian last pair hung on through a gripping final fifteen minutes. Rain spoilt the Oval Test, what play there was being graced by a serene century from Merchant.

There was great interest in these matches as there had been in many of the county games, and good crowds seemed to justify the decision to let sleeping dogs lie in terms of cricketing reform. People were naturally anxious to watch cricket again, and they turned out in fine numbers, despite the miserable weather. It is ironic that the summer of 1940, the first for a generation when no first-class play had been possible, had been dry and sunny, and that 1946, when cricket was resumed, suffered such wetness as caused pundits to compare it with the dreadful summers of 1879, 1888 and 1902, although 1879, when there were scarcely three consecutive good days, is normally felt to have been the worst ever.

Where the Indians were most lacking was in the quality of their pace attack, for frankly they had no one of high or effective speed. This meant, especially in so soggy a season, that the top English batsmen had little chance to reorientate themselves to the hazards of sheer velocity of the kind they were shortly to experience in Australia. With Farnes sadly dead, and with Bowes and Voce no longer as fiery, after the arduous toll of warfare, there was precious little speed of any consequence on the county circuit. There was no young crop of strapping, zestful fast bowlers to test reflexes perhaps dulled by six lost summers and two or three lost winter tours.

To complete the air of *déjà vu*, the other traditional matches were resumed. The Gentlemen and Players match was usually a helpful guide to the state of English cricket but it, too, was marred by rain. The heavy showers made spiteful a wicket upon which the Players, chiefly through a Washbrook century, had earlier scored fruitfully, and the Gentlemen were quickly dispatched twice. W. R. Hammond, with 70, was the only amateur to shine – so there was no new facts to be learned there. Much the same might be said of the University match. The one lone star was the excellent New Zealand left-hander Martin Donnelly. He scored more runs in a season for Oxford than anyone save the Nawab of Pataudi himself years before, and his 142 demolished an extremely modest Cambridge XI. D. H. Macindoe, captain and main bowler, and Richard Sale, the opening bat, were his chief assistants, but there appeared to be a lack of real immediate talent among the undergraduates. However, it was a wholesome vengeance for the Dark Blues. Without a ground, with players scattered and with fewer games than their rivals, they had had by far the worst of the one-day wartime encounters.

It must also be emphasised that, good as it was to have cricket under way again, conditions were by no means ideal. Travel was not easy and hotel life was not glamorous. Jack Fallows, the Lancashire captain, is reported as having been faced with strategic decisions off as well as on the field, such as whether the bowlers or the batsmen should have the two or three fried eggs available at breakfast. Many critics felt that, partly because neither men nor grounds had recovered sufficiently, the standards of play were not as good as in the 1930s.

In summary, and although the 1946 was welcome and enjoyable, it did not offer enough opportunity for the continual and appropriate rehabilitation of senior English cricket. The general post-war shabbiness of conditions; the wet summer; the lack of practice against fast bowling; the reliance on the old guard and the almost complete absence of fresh talent; and perhaps the refusal to invigorate the game with some sparkling and original principles – these were the factors that made 1946 a season of rather ordinary, even dull, character, with no hint at all of what 1947 would bring by way of fulsome delights. For the realistic, however, there was only too lucid a glimpse of what would happen to the English team when it toured Australia during the winter of 1946–47.

Effectively, the roots of misfortune went back much longer than the wartime years, and, indeed, might be traced as early as the time of the First World War. It was about that era, not least because of the profound influence of the first war on cricket and cricketers, that the sacrosanct nature of 'the holy game' allowed it to become rigidified. It amounts to a remarkable cultural paradox. It became the mannered fashion to associate the Victorians with stolidity and complacency, and to observe in the doings of 20th-century man a surging vein of progressive thought and love of experiment. Whatever the truth of this dichotomy in other fields (and one might suggest that it is almost everywhere a misleading interpretation), in cricket it is a palpable nonsense. The Victorian cricket authorities recognised that the game was organic and acknowledged that it should alter as circumstances changed. There were plenty of controversies, of course, but overall the basic reforms in the method and structure of cricket were continuous.

By the end of the Edwardian age, the myth had developed of

cricket's pastoral simplicity and unchanging rite, and its adherents adopted a somewhat unhealthy posture of allegiance to the sacred cause. This worship of a sporting graven image, this insistence that cricket was a finished and rounded corpus that brooked no word of heretical criticism, persisted to the extent that, in 1946, first-class cricket was fundamentally the same in mode and construct as fifty years before. A telling illustration is the format of the County Championship. Although the points system and the detail of match regulation had been and would be altered with cavalier abandon, the basic doctrine endured untrammelled. It was as if the design of the vestments or the covers of the pews might be changed time and time again, but no one dare broach the supreme truth and authority of the underlying dogma. After all, only one novitiate – Glamorgan –had forced itself into the druidic circle since the First World War, and that was in 1921; only one other youthful aspirant – Northamptonshire, in 1905 – had broken in during this century, although Durham has now been offered baptism. Equally significantly, no priest has been unfrocked or excommunicated since the late 19th century.

That is a degree of rigidity which borders on the unwholesome, and there can be little doubt that the compulsory pause of the Second World War offered the establishment a tempting opportunity to relate cricket's schema more relevantly to radically transformed socio-economic conditions, an opportunity it foolishly ignored. By its faithful reflection and celebration of the mores and mechanics of its score and more predecessors, the 1946 season thus exhibited an awful and pious smugness.

2

The Australian Warning

The national elation at the end of a desperate and frightening war was offset by debilitating effects. Only a third of the nation's export trade, measured by pre-war values, remained, and the merchant fleet which might have carried it was now only two-thirds the strength it had been in 1939. It was estimated that a tenth of the country's wealth and resource had been destroyed by war. The nation's debts were almost £50 billion. In 1946 alone Great Britain spent £300 million more overseas than she earned. By a sad wryness there was an early end to the Japanese war, which pundits had expected to continue for another twelve or eighteen months before the two great atomic explosions at Hiroshima and Nagasaki. American aid stopped abruptly on VJ Day, while already supplies had been diverted to continental Europe which required urgent succour for its stricken millions. Rationing persisted until the 1950s, and indeed bread and cakes were not rationed until *after* the war. Another repercussion of the sudden end to the Japanese war was that there was little scope to decelerate either demobilisation or the war economy. This, coupled in some views with outdated methods of production, management and labour relations, made for a somewhat uneasy resumption to peace-time economics.

Britain had certainly enjoyed her finest hour, and few would quarrel with A. J. P. Taylor's conclusion that, in this 'people's war in the most literal sense', the British citizenry 'came of age'. But the price of the sacrifice was complete exhaustion, and, from another angle, an absolute change of diplomatic status. It had been Britain's task to hold the breach against the Fascist threat, and this had been achieved. However, as the war spread from a continental to a global arena, the end of Britain's role as a world power was apparent. The German invasion of Russia and the Japanese onslaught of Pearl

Harbor, although marking the beginning of world opposition to the Axis states, at the same time denoted the emergence of the USA and USSR as the superpowers of the future. That curt diversion of American aid from British to European shores was in part compassionate in motive, but it was also an opening salvo in the cold war, as the USA attempted to press her influence in a region where she had never before been much interested, but where Soviet hegemony had suddenly extended with, in transatlantic eyes, alarming speed.

It was to be some years before the British establishment became used to the notion of being a second-class power; indeed, it could be soundly argued that it still has not. The fiasco of Suez and the jingoism of the Falklands War, as well as the antics of some press and politicians over Britain's place in Europe and her contribution to nuclear defence or to the 1991 Gulf War, are evidence of the failure to comprehend that the United Kingdom is now more in the category of an Austria or a Norway – and to be grateful for it.

If by 1991 the powers-that-be have not seen the light, then, flushed with the triumph of victory, it was scarcely likely that their sense of perspective would have been particularly lucid in 1946; and this surely applied to cricket as an exemplar of national life.

Barely had the Japanese surrender been accepted when the Australian cricketing authorities were urging MCC to send forth a touring party. MCC was reluctant to do so, but the invitation was strongly pressed, and supported by Dr H. V. Evatt, the Australian premier. By the new year of 1946 the trip had been agreed.

The discussion of this invitation makes for interesting reading. Some who recalled or had studied the MCC tour to the Antipodes of 1920–21, following closely on the end of the First World War, were cool in their response. W. W. Armstrong's Australians had won all five Tests with some comfort, and the moral drawn was that a year or so of preparation was essential now before taking on the might of the Australians. In a sense, the proponents of this view were right, or at least they were more realistic than their opponents, who scoffed at such timidity, banged the patriotic drum, and insisted that English cricket should not be so feeble-minded. England had talented batsmen, and they would lord it over the Australians as 'the Few' had proudly fought the Luftwaffe.

A third opinion might have been lodged. Both the preceding cases (it might have argued) were misleading in mantling the proceedings with a vaster solemnity than a mere sport warranted. Those were sanest who felt that, for reasons of goodwill and good fellowship, and as a gesture of appreciation to Australia, who had made heavy sacrifices for the mother country, a tour could do no harm.

In social and political terms, moreover, the 1946–47 tour was outstandingly successful. The MCC players were extremely well received and immensely popular wherever they visited. It was, after all, the first such trip since G. O. Allen's tour all of ten years before and, of course, after accepting the Indians as visitors in 1946, it would have seemed churlish not to have acceded to so eager an invitation. Crowds were huge, and one not unimportant measure of the tour's success was a share of the profits which topped £50,000. What was, as ever, dismaying was that, having engaged on such a venture for what could decently be interpreted as amiable reasons, critics could not forbear, according to geographic disposition, to rejoice fervently or fault-find acrimoniously – for, in playing terms, Australia were supreme and England a little abject.

Needless to say, Australia had been disrupted by the war; first through the dispatch of many valiant soldiers and airmen to many theatres of war, and next by the more imminent threat of Japanese aggression in the Pacific. That said, cricket was sustained perhaps a little less fitfully than in the United Kingdom. At government bidding the Sheffield Shield tournament was played out in the 1939–40 season, with Bradman dominant as ever and with New South Wales the victors. In 1940–41 there was no such contest, but eleven first-class matches were arranged, quite a considerable number when one remembers that the four states only then played half a dozen matches each in the Sheffield Shield. What is interesting about these two early wartime seasons is the emergence of young players who would play their role in Australia's post-war success. The opening batsmen, Sidney Barnes and Arthur Morris, both of New South Wales, were outstanding, while names such as Colin McCool, Ron Saggers and Cecil Pepper also attracted due attention.

In 1941–42, an inter-state Patriotic Cup was planned, which had a most complex scoring system, but only one of the eighteen games was completed. The government cancelled the rest because of the hazard posed by the Japanese, and eleven exhibition matches, which did not prove too popular, were substituted. There were complaints that, in Australia as in England, the towel had been thrown in too soon, and that, with the Japanese not too adjacent, with sufficient players still available, and with a hard-working populace in need of a wholesome break, this abandonment was premature. In the United States President Roosevelt guaranteed that men and materials were available to keep baseball going, his astute instincts informing him that high-class relaxation was a critical factor in the war effort. To preserve political balance, one should also note that in the Soviet Union, under Stalin, 300,000 footballers were busy in various competitions even as the grim siege of Stalingrad took place.

Still, cricket continued in Australia at a reasonable level, while those Australian cricketers who trooped to the colours often found themselves donning whites in foreign climes. The Royal Australian Air Force were especially striking as a cricket team in England, and during 1945 some forty of the hundred main matches played in this country included service teams representative of Australia or New Zealand. This meant that, for the future, many young cricketers were gaining first-hand experience not only of English conditions but of senior English players.

This process reached its apotheosis in the Victory Tests of 1945, that series of five fine engagements, topped off with a heady and vivid match between England and the Dominions, which still tugs at the heartstrings of those thousands whose earliest memories of first-class cricket were then formed. Indeed, the opening Test, started on 19 May, was the first recognised first-class game to be played in England since September 1939. The Australians were captained by Lindsay Hassett, one of only a handful of soldiers in the squad – J. E. Cheetham, Cec Pepper and R. S. Whitington were the others. Given the particular exigencies of war, Australian airmen were much more in evidence, than army personnel, so much so that Hassett, a warrant officer, found himself leading a side chiefly composed of air force officers. Against what on paper were very strong English XIs, they won two, lost two and drew one, and to the delight of enormous crowds the cricket was lively and imaginative at almost all stages of all the games.

It was velvet luxury; but the more level-headed spotted through the joyous brio a nasty flaw. Verity and Farnes were mournfully dead; Bill Bowes was a just-released prisoner of war; and Denis Compton and Joe Hardstaff were in India. But, apart from these, England put staunch sides in the field, including the likes of Hammond, Edrich, Fishlock, Hutton, Pollard and Wright, all of whom were destined to tour Australia in 1946–47. Youngsters were offered a chance, but they were outgunned: Hon. L. R. White, the Etonian bat, later to play for Middlesex, D. B. Carr of Repton, soon to captain Derbyshire and, indeed, England, and later to become Secretary of MCC, and J. G. Dewes, of Cambridge, Middlesex and the Royal Navy, were tried in the third Test and found severely wanting.

Conversely, Hassett was Australia's only capped player. It was in these matches that the ebullient Keith Miller came to international attention with his graphic all-round displays, and these two would, of course, grace Australian sides for many seasons to come. Yet they were the only ones. What was or should have been a cause of English anxiety was that, by the exacting criteria of Australian post-war cricket, none of their colleagues would make the international grade. Some became efficient state players; some joined English county or league teams; some never sought or found a place in first-class cricket. These were names that were bandied liberally about in the summer of 1945: the skilful all-rounder, Christofani; batsmen such as Workman; a wicket-keeper as accomplished as Sismey; bowlers quick like Roper, or slow like Pettiford – such as these do not even warrant the meagre acknowledgement of their births being included in *Wisden*. Others like D. K. Carmody, of the famed umbrella slip field, R. S. Whitington, the writer, or Cec Pepper, who found fortune in the British Isles, have been better remembered; but the main trait of that attractive young Australian team was their relative lack of individual success after 1945.

We have already touched on the wrong lessons that were learned from wartime cricket, and the Victory Tests, never humdrum, always cheerful, played in a spontaneous mood of exuberant celebration and touched with the sparkle of carnival, contributed to this misspent schooling. It was the ingredients of these games which were so entrancing, rather than the format in which they were played. The cricketing authorities read two false omens into them: one was to do with the state of English cricket and the other was to do with the state of English cricketers. The forthcoming journey to Australia was to offer other such portents, some of which, again, were not to be usefully interpreted.

On 31 August 1946 the party, managed by Major Rupert Howard, the Lancashire secretary, departed from Southampton aboard the RMS *Stirling Castle*. It was a government-chartered ship and it was pronounced 'dry', which cannot have pleased some of its sporting passengers. A sign of the war years, its main task was to carry 200 war-brides to be reunited with their ex-service Australian husbands. This offered some pleasure, according to his kindly obituarist, to Bill Edrich, whose fascination for the ladies was legendary. The boat docked, as was traditional, at Fremantle, and the team were enthusiastically received. The voyage, the sun, and above all the switch from English rations to Australian hospitality was a boon, in so far as all the players were in excellent health, but there were drawbacks, for it was reported that everyone had put on weight, the fast bowlers more than anyone.

MCC won only one first-class match in Australia, and that was a sound thrashing of the champion state, Victoria, who went down by 244 runs: Compton and Hutton scored centuries, and Wright took ten wickets in the match. Three country XIs were beaten, and, apart from the three Test defeats, every other fixture was drawn. Although, with two drawn Tests, MCC in 1946–47 seemed to have made marginally better progress than the whitewashed team of 1920–21, Australia always had the definitive upper hand.

The Tests were contested over six days, instead of the previous practice of playing on until a definite result was obtained, so that the drawn Tests were the first on Australian soil in official Ashes games. England had, on their side, agreed to five-day Tests of six hours daily for the next Australian visit to Britain.

The first Test was at Brisbane, and England lost by the heavy margin of 332 runs. They endured two pieces of misfortune, the one collective, the other of a more individual nature. Whereas Australia batted comfortably in conditions which were stifling for the fielding side, England then found themselves batting in each innings following a thunderstorm. Thus the Australians made their highest-ever score – 645 – on their own soil, while Bradman and Hassett added 276 for the third wicket, still the record for the Ashes. Then England fell for 141 and 172, with Miller taking 7 for 60 in the first innings and the left-handed Toshack ten wickets in the match. It was the home side's first win in Queensland against England.

The personal incident concerned Bradman. He seemed unsure both as to form and health, and came to Brisbane as if on trial. There were many ready to proclaim him finished, and after Morris had disappeared in Bedser's second over, his preliminary overtures were flustered and uneasy. Barnes tried to shield him, itself an extraordinary statement, and in forty minutes Bradman had scored only 7. Barnes was soon dismissed and, with the board showing 74–2 and Bradman 28, a ball from Voce flew to the secure grasp of Ikin at second slip. Bradman stood his ground, presuming perhaps that he had sharply jabbed the ball from the ground. The English fielders then confidently appealed, the more so in that a fairer-minded cricketer than Ikin would have been difficult to discover. Bradman survived the appeal, and went on to make 187, his only century at Brisbane against England. Thus on the first morning of the first Test occurred an incident which was to have momentous impact, for there was a general belief that an initial failure might have caused Bradman to have retired from Test cricket immediately. Whether or not he would have taken, or been asked to take, that step, the matter of a catch at second slip is not easily explained away. One might criticise Bradman for not walking at the instigation of, one would like to believe, sporting fielders; on the larger plane, one must worry about the public and press build-up that might have created so stressful a pressure that failure could be so painful an option.

The teams contested the second Test at Sydney just before what was to prove an unhappy Christmas for the England party. Australia won by an innings and 33 runs, thus matching their success during Stoddart's tour in 1897–98 when two successive Tests had also been won by an innings. On a placid pitch, and with Lindwall not available, England succumbed to the spin of Johnson and McCool, with only Edrich and Ikin showing promise. Despite a pronounced limp, Bradman then shared with Barnes what remains the world's highest fifth-wicket stand. Each scored exactly 234; each fell when the score was 564; and 405 were added. Despite an Edrich century and improved batting all round, the Australians had no need to bat a second time. There were compensations. The fielding was a little better than at Brisbane where at least five expensive chances had gone begging. Paul Gibb (who had dropped McCool when he had barely scored: he made 95) was rested, and, in his first Test, Godfrey Evans conceded not a bye in that massive total of 659, for the Australians again made their highest home Test score. It was the start of an exuberantly potent international career. All agreed that Wright's 1–169 was a travesty of cricketing justice, so fizzingly accurate had been his bowling, but England had in reality perished with all hands.

The new year Test was at Melbourne. Not only was it the first drawn Ashes Test, it was also only the third draw on Australian soil, the other two having been gained by Alfred Shaw's party in 1881–82. England had ill luck with injuries both before and early in the game, which weakened the bowling considerably, and English voices were also raised in complaint about two or three umpiring decisions. Nonetheless, the teams were well matched on the first innings, but, with late batting of dazzling violence, Lindwall and Tallon scored 100 and 92 respectively and left England too great a task. A century from Washbrook and continued support from Yardley, the emergent all-rounder, saved England further embarrassment.

A month later the fourth Test was played at Adelaide and this too was drawn. Batting dominated throughout a week of torrid heat. Hutton and Washbrook began each innings with a century opening stand, and Compton scored a century in each innings. This was emulated by Arthur Morris (the first such occasion for an Australian in a home Test), while Miller entertained with 141, although he was dropped three times having reached his hundred. England flirted with disaster in the second innings, but Compton and Evans, the latter batting ninety-five minutes before scoring, saved England's bacon.

The final Test was back at Sydney and the Australians won an attractive game by five wickets. Hammond, whose fibrositis was a nuisance in the fourth Test and whose form was poor, stood down, and Yardley captained England thoughtfully and carefully. There was more bad luck, for Hutton, on 122, retired ill with tonsillitis, and could not bat at all in the second innings. There was more bad fielding, in particular the simple dropping by Edrich of Bradman when he was 2 the second time round. He went on to score 63 and steered Australia almost home. Heavy rain had produced a much more balanced wicket, and the scoring was less gargantuan. England led on the first innings, in spite of Lindwall's shattering analysis of 7 for 63: Wright at last earned merited reward with his splendid 7 for 105, and Bedser continued his consistent ways. However, without Hutton and with only Compton showing any spirited response, England fell to the trickery of McCool, and the Australians required only little more than 200 for their third victory of the series.

A reduced party then travelled by flying-boat to New Zealand, where Wellington and Auckland were easily accounted for, and where the match with Otago ended, midst tingling excitement, in a draw. Atrocious weather ruined the one Test match, and it was scarcely possible to complete an innings each. His many friends were overjoyed to watch Hammond score a grand and nostalgic 79 in what turned out to be his last Test appearance and his last innings before announcing his retirement from first-class cricket. It was an eminently satisfactory farewell, and pleased those who had feared that this most imperious of cricketers would limp in tepid, humbled fashion from the game he had adorned. What the less romantic spotted was that the English bowling had taken something of a caning, with Walter Hadlee notching his first Test century, and Bert Sutcliffe, the handsome left-hander, joining him with a promising half century. Similarly, the quick bowling of Jack Cowie, who took six of England's seven wickets to fall, reminded one and all that fast bowling was not especially relished by the England batsmen.

We read the dispatches of these happenings, cabled for inclusion in newspapers still emaciated by paper rationing, and we listened with sober attention to the squeaky, crackly commentaries on the 'wireless'. The sombre tidings arrived during dismal winter mornings, with home and streets still dark and chill. Spluttering coal fires, barely yet alight, were the lot of most in those stone-cold houses, as cricket-lovers took stock of the relentlessly bad news.

Unfriendly fortune with injuries and illness, with umpires, with weather, and with near-miss bowling was one factor, and that was not to be dismissed, but still the gap between the two sides was very wide. It was most noticeable in the opposing attacks for, valiantly and expertly although Bedser and Wright tried, they were not adequately supported. This meant that they were overworked, and Wright, much admired by Australians for his artistry, suffered accordingly. The wickets were not to Alec Bedser's liking, but he persevered adamantly, while Yardley contributed more and more as the long tour wound on. Voce, once the scourge of Australia, took no wickets and Peter Smith took only 2, while neither Pollard nor James Langridge played in an Australian Test. Bill Edrich, with 9 wickets, was the fourth best bowler, and all these figures underlined the urgent need for at least one very quick bowler and a classic left-hand spinner – mordantly, it must be said, a Farnes and a Verity. Conversely, Australia fielded an attack for all seasons, and, although the headlines yelled of Lindwall and Miller, the associated spin and medium bowling was extremely penetrative. Ray Lindwall had 18 victims, and his partner, Keith Miller, 16, but Colin McCool took 17 wickets, Ernie Toshack 17, Ian Johnson 10 and Bruce Dooland 8. The success was thus deservedly spread over a most comprehensive array of gifted bowlers.

The English fielding lapses have already been noted, and against that must be mentioned the athletic prowess in the field of the Australians. Their catching and throwing was of high order. The only parity was behind the stumps, where the rare élan of Evans paralleled the technical excellence of Tallon. As Lindwall and Tallon also demonstrated, the Australians batted well down the order, only Toshack being feeble as a batsman. England normally picked three without much batting acumen.

At a personal level, a gulf emerged between Bradman and Hammond, both as batsmen and as captains. Bradman seemed to be the astuter as a strategist, while Hammond was often criticised for some of his tactical decisions and for a general lack of inspiration. Even then, let alone later in retrospect, was it difficult to assess how much this was personal expertise and how much the steamroller effect of success. Bradman had the better players who performed with frequent brilliance; he started a sickly man and blossomed into strong health and long scores. Hammond, with the poorer players, could not motivate them zestfully; his own form deteriorated and he fell ill. That said, he was served with respectful loyalty, and the usual tales of ill-discipline and easy living, which are often appended to an ailing tourist party, were wide of their mark.

Certainly the gap was a crucial one. Hammond's 168 runs, average 21, is definitely puny alongside Bradman's 680, average 97. This is the more telling when the rest of the batting is compared, for here England and Australia most closely approached in equity. Miller, Barnes and Morris each averaged over 70, with McCool on 54 and Hassett on 47, but these achievements were obtained against inferior bowling. Even against the much more formidable Australian attack, Hutton and Compton, after poorish starts, had averages of 52 and 51 respectively, while Edrich, a late selection, averaged 46. Washbrook, whose fielding was outstanding, had an average of 36, although he was much more dour of mien than on his native heath; the up-and-coming Yardley had an average of 31; Hardstaff, who had few chances, scored 67 in his only Test. Present day cricket fans would find much to applaud if four or five English batsmen were performing in that manner now. Gibb, Fishlock, and James Langridge disappointed, although injury had a part to play in regard of the last. Ikin, whose fielding was exemplary (he took twenty-four catches in first-class matches, easily the best record), batted diligently, but was bowled sparingly and without success, so that he never evolved into a passable international all-rounder.

England did pass the 250 mark in seven out of ten innings; there was rarely an abject collapse as such: it was rather that the scores looked, and were, sorry when set against the huge compilations of the home team. No less than eleven of the Australians averaged over 20, a remarkable tribute to their lack of tail, and perhaps also a token of the inadequacies of the English bowling.

Although there had been misgivings about the tour, the gravity of the discrepancy between the two teams shook the confidence of the cricketing world at home. Because, dating from that winter season, several of the Australians became household names, it is now forgotten that the series matched hardened veterans with tyros. Of the seventeen MCC choices, only Yardley and Evans were uncapped on sailing, although two or three, such as Bedser, Ikin and Smith, had only reached that hallowed distinction courtesy of the visiting Indians in 1946. However, seven of the group had played in Tests against Australia, and the party teemed with experience. Only Bradman and Hassett had played in Tests against England. What amounted to a bunch of unknowns found sudden fame and, coaxed and spurred by Bradman, they coalesced into a much more coherent task force than England. Seven of them shared ten Test centuries, against England's four sharing five, and in Keith Miller, who was of course known to English crowds from his wartime appearance, the Australians had the pick of a crop of excellent all-rounders.

Whereas the mid-1920s had been years of drought for English cricketers – no one who had been born then, bar Graveney, gained English caps in double figures – Australia managed to rear a fruitful crop. Beginning with Johnson in 1918, and Miller in 1919, one finds Lindwall born in 1921, Morris in 1922 and, looking to the future, Neil Harvey in 1928. Others – Barnes, Toshack and Tallon, for instance – were of a slightly older vintage, but they seemed to have kept their cricketing acts together during the war years more efficiently than their English counterparts. Ultimately, the England of the late 1930s was vanquished by the new-wave Australians of the 1940s.

One would have benefited from brighter news at home in England. The Labour government, led by Clement Attlee, was embarked on its courageous programme of effecting 'the silent revolution', in terms of enhanced economic control and social reform, at precisely the time Britain was burdened with post-war stresses. The promised plans for public ownership were already started, with nationalisation of key industries, and the groundwork for a more just system of welfare had been laid. Of course, while recognising the need to persist with rationing and other regimens, people were tired of drabness and half-empty shops, and yet dollar exports had to be maximised for a country virtually bankrupt.

The cruellest blow to government and nation was the winter of 1946–47, which contrived to be the harshest for nearly seventy years. From the middle of December, a Britain already desperately short of coal faced paralysis. Snow fell and fell and, by the time the fourth Test was being played at Adelaide in scorching temperatures, the entire country was deeply covered and frozen solid. It was the worst kind of freak winter, and it could not have chosen a more unfortunate time. Shipping was slowed down and sometimes immobilised; for days something like half London's commuters could not reach the city; schools and other public buildings closed; there were gas and electricity cuts. Soon there was no electricity for industry over huge tracts of the nation, and two million men were out of work. The use of electric fires was banned at certain times of the day, and television was suspended.

As late as March the blizzards and frosts continued, with 300 main roads still impassable; Scotland cut off completely; houses buried in thirty-foot drifts; livestock dead and crops ruined. Then, in the middle of March, came sudden thaw. The resultant floods, a tempest loosing a swirling deluge, inundated three-quarters of a million acres of farming land, drowned sheep and cattle in their thousands, and soaked the homes and townships of many unfortunate citizens. The restrictions which had to be imposed to counter the impact of these disasters, arriving as they did on top of other troubles, were as stringent as any known in the war itself. Up went the posters: 'We Work or Want' – and it was not idle propaganda. Imports were drastically curtailed, and there were many victims, from petrol to American films. With the timber shortage, the newspapers reverted to four pages again.

The people grumbled and tried to make the best of a bad job, and some of the wartime mood of indomitable fortitude surfaced. Clothing and footwear were still in short supply, and the weeks of cold, unnatural almost in its persistent chill, were numbing. These climatic scourges hit Britain with the force of Old Testament retribution, and, from flooded London Underground track to heavy snow in the Channel Islands, there was no relief for anyone. Many alive in 1947 may have forgotten the bleak detail of that cheerless existence: not one of them has forgotten the cold, and its icy grip.

Away in Australia there was little of good cheer, except possibly the fact that our favourites were gaining in abrasive experience, eating off the fat of the land, and generally enjoying a healthy break from British austerity. As cricketers might say, they 'wintered well'; and several of those hard-pressed heroes were to return to these shores wiser and fitter sportsmen. It is interesting to observe how many of them were to be the stars of the glorious summer of 1947, and to ponder on whether their disappointing winter in the antipodes did, in fact, put them on their mettle for the coming cricketing pageant.

PART TWO

The Season

3

The Opening Shots

The Australian débâcle, perhaps because remote in place and sprinkled with real compensations, was put to the back of cricket's collective mind as April neared its end and the county staffs reported for duty.

Two years had passed since the end of the war, but it was still difficult to spot talented newcomers. Trevor Bailey, a Cambridge Blue in 1947, played ten matches for Essex, and contrived to be first in their batting averages and second in the bowling. Tony Pawson, of Winchester and Oxford University, also did well for Kent towards the end of the season, while Maurice Tremlett, the all-rounder who had promised well in wartime cricket, made an impressive start to his Somerset career. Middlesex saw the beginning of Norman Hever's conscientious spell as a fast-medium bowler, albeit mostly with Glamorgan, and a Finchley 17-year-old, the leg-spinner Ian Bedford, enjoyed a satisfactory debut. Across the river at the Oval, D. G. W. Fletcher delighted with close on 2,000 runs in his opening season. He brilliantly took his chance when Fishlock, who had not had much luck in Australia, was struck down by appendicitis in May. However, the chief revelation of the season was Andy Sandham's discovery of Jim Laker who, having caused some stirrings in the Middle East during his war service there, was bowling his off-breaks for Catford in London club cricket. He topped the Surrey averages with 66 wickets.

T. L. Pritchard, the New Zealand fast bowler, sharpened up the Warwickshire attack and took 87 wickets in the Championship, but he could scarcely be regarded as home-grown talent. In the north there was much excitement generated over the arrival of Ken Cranston, the lively Liverpool all-rounder, whose epic little tale was to be one of many recorded throughout 1947, but across the

Pennines it was more a case of retirements than recruitments. Maurice Leyland, Wilf Barber and Cyril Turner had all finished at the end of 1946, and something of a hole was left in the Yorkshire batting. The main debut of note was that of D. V. Brennan, something of a curio as an amateur wicket-keeper, but who was to offer secure consistency in that position for the next seven seasons.

There were, of course, other newcomers, and still others who had been on the fringe of their county side, and for whom 1947 was to be their first full season and major breakthrough into the top echelon of cricket. One might recall, for instance, and solely from the Yorkshire ranks, the bowling of Johnny Wardle and the handsome stroke-play of G. A. Smithson, soon to transfer to Leicestershire. Each had made his debut in 1946; each would consolidate a first-team place in 1947; each would be selected for the 1947–48 tour of the West Indies.

There was, then, enough to allow grounds for pleasurable anticipation, and yet, as the season unfolded, it would be observed that, as in 1946 and on the Australian winter tour, it would be the pre-war stars who once more found themselves in the limelight.

A word is perhaps necessary, or at least useful, about the playing conditions for the County Championship. These had been changed in the details, if rarely in the fundamentals, with bewildering complexity between the wars, but the pre-war system was more or less inherited intact, and for the next decade or so it remained constant. This was a tribute both to the conservatism and to the enlightenment of the authorities: they were naturally anxious not to keep making adjustments, and in truth frequent and peripheral alterations had done nothing much to improve either the playing or the watching of the game.

The 'rationalisation scheme' announced before the war had now taken proper effect, and the absurdities of counties having fixture lists of varying lengths and strengths was over. In 1947, as in 1946, everyone played twenty-six games, equally divided home and away, six counties once, and the other ten twice, home and away. It was still not ideal in the Football League sense of an even competition, with all counties meeting each other twice, but it was a major improvement on many pre-war seasons. Twelve points went to the county winning a match. In a drawn match, the county leading on the first innings took four points. However, if the county eventually lost the match, but had a first innings lead, the four points were retained. If play was restricted to the third day, and a draw resulted, there was a bounty of eight points for the first innings leaders, while two points apiece were awarded both counties in a drawn match where the first innings scores were level – again, these two points were retained by a county losing the match.

Although this system endured more than any thus far in the variegated history of Championship scoring, it had its defects and it had its critics. Too many sides settled, either by conscious resolve or silent agreement, to battle out the quest for first innings points. The system of bowling and batting points of the modern dispensation does at least offer the chance of profit to both attack and defence equally and continuously, but the older mode sometimes made for a bleak struggle over two or, occasionally, three days, with few pickings left for the final hours. Many found it indefensible that a losing side could bank any points at all – indeed, it might have been fairer merely to award four points for first innings lead, so that a winning team could have ended with a tally of sixteen. As it was, a county perhaps lucky to have gained a first innings lead, and then losing very heavily, fared better than a county which fought a close-run draw, possibly near to victory, but failing to obtain that first innings advantage. In 1947 there were to be no less than twenty-four instances of a losing team getting those four points, including one where Essex were awarded two points for a tie in the first innings during a losing encounter. This compared with sixty-one occasions when, in a drawn game, a county had four points for first innings advantage. We shall see whether this flaw in the scoring, as it was regarded by many critics, was to affect the outcome.

Thus was the slate rendered and made ready for the tourney, perhaps the most celebrated in the history of the Championship, and a series of pulsating games was interspersed with some excellent Test cricket. England's opponents in 1947 were the South Africans. It was twelve years since their last visit. In 1935 H. F. Wade's team had played five Tests against Wyatt's England side, winning one and drawing four. This single victory, happily for the South Africans at Lord's, gave them the rubber in a series which demonstrated that three-day Tests were now too brief for so accomplished a cricketing nation. Hammond had then led a strong MCC party to South Africa in 1938–39; in fact it was the first time that the South Africans had received the strongest available touring side from England. On placid wickets the rubber was reversed, with England this time winning one Test and the other four being drawn. Alan Melville captained the South Africans, and it was he who now captained them on English shores in 1947.

The illiberal regime which was to play havoc with South Africa's place in world affairs, as well as bring shame and suffering to her domestic life, was not yet implanted. Although South Africa was not then the intolerant and divided nation of later years, one must also allow for some lack of awareness of the poison of racial subservience among the watching English spectators. After all, the freeing of many races from the British imperial yoke had scarcely begun. On the other hand, the South Africans were extremely popular. Their cricketers, young, eager and very sporting, were well received, as had been the case with preceding tourists from the Union. They were, according to the convention of their country, highly talented club cricketers, amateur in character and mien. Many had firm affinities with Britain – Melville had captained Oxford University in 1931 and 1932, for instance – and, of course, no one forgot that South Africa's part in the war had been sizeable and was much appreciated in the home country. Nonetheless, it should not be forgotten that the non-white bowler, C. B. Llewellyn, who had played for South Africa before the First World War, had been cruelly treated by his white colleagues.

Those undertones were either unknown or not broadcast in 1947, and the South Africans, never regarded with anything like the same fierce rivalry as the Australians, were welcomed in the most friendly fashion, and responded in chivalrous manner. They were to grace the English summer with their skills and sportsmanship.

Rightly and accurately, the 1947 season is closely identified with Denis Compton and Bill Edrich. With the passage of the years the story has come to sound something like this: Compton and Edrich swept Middlesex to a scorching and runaway Championship win and England to glorious triumph in the Tests, all against the background of an outstandingly hot summer. The kernel of veracity is there, for by and large these matters came about in that way.

Nonetheless, the hard facts have been smeared with traces of mythical balm.

First, Middlesex did not bask so easily in relaxed dominance. Gloucestershire gave them a good run for their money. In the middle of August they lost an exciting match to the eventual champions, but even then it was the end of that month before Middlesex were assured of their splendid success. Lancashire, who lost only once, were also in some contention, so that this was no one-horse race. Second, and although England won three Tests and drew two, the South Africans suffered whatever ill-luck was going, and might easily have won two of this interesting set of matches. Third, the weather was not unfailingly sunny, as the luckless South Africans found once or twice to their cost. While the collective memory has etched the picture of day after day of cloudless sky, there were rainy and chilly spells.

These were especially prominent in the opening days of the season. What happened was that eventually, and apart from a couple of breaks in July, the summer settled into one of scorching intensity. August was hot and humid, and tiringly so. People remember this and forget the earlier moistness and cold. The sharp winds of April and May signalled the tailpiece of a miserable winter. It really was abrasively unseasonable, with buffeting gusts of air to make one shiver. Because of the heavy snowfalls, it had been an extremely wet winter, and one which maintained its dampness into May. Thus cricket grounds were sodden, and some had been flooded. Worcester's ground at New Road had experienced its worst flooding from the overswollen Severn for as far back as men could remember, and there had even been fears that the opening match against the South Africans there might not have been possible.

Not that the sunshine, when it came, was unfailingly beneficial. There was too much of it, and the occasional thunderstorms grumbled ominously over a tired and worn nation. Fruit was still in short supply from overseas, and the now ubiquitous refrigerator was rarely to be seen, so that cooling and preserving food was at a discount. Food was in poor supply, perhaps as little being available as at any time since the beginning of the war. The basic petrol ration was abolished, foreign travel suspended and even the clothing ration coupons reduced. It became a criminal offence to switch on a gas or electric fire during the summer months, although to be sure the climatic conditions meant that only bravado might have motivated the shameless law-breaker so to offend.

With that irksome trait for which British weather is infamous, drought promptly followed the floods. The dry spell especially hit the Welsh hills, and the water supply of Manchester, to the grim delight of those many whose cricketing memories of Old Trafford were damp in the extreme, was almost exhausted. The drought also caused a polio scare, and children were warned to keep away from the swimming baths, one of the few local sources of relief from the increasingly intemperate sun.

On Wednesday 30 April the South Africans opened this momentous season in freezingly bitter conditions, and on a pitch which, scarcely recovered from the deluge, was perilous to batsmen. As a year before, when they defeated the Indians, Worcestershire now beat the South Africans in a low-scoring encounter. The tourists began encouragingly and soon had Worcester reeling at 37 for 5. The light was grey and there were flurries of rain and even sleet, but Ronnie Bird struggled to 79, the only score above 28 in the game and his own career best, amazingly, given the adverse circumstances. Worcester reached 202. In their second attempt, and despite a sturdy opening stand of 44 from the Cooper brothers, they collapsed to 111, Athol Rowan, the off-spinner, settling into a rhythm of acute turn which brought him five wickets in each innings. It was enough for the South Africans, who could only muster 167 and 107 in each innings, and Worcester won quite comfortably by 39 runs. The canny Reg Perks bowled his medium pace intelligently in the first innings and took 5 wickets, while Dick Howorth, his languid left-arm spin floating indolently away, bemused his opponents in the second. He took 6 for 38, whilst Peter Jackson loaned competent support with 4 wickets in each innings. The top South African score the second time round was 16.

If ever experienced know-how and local knowledge had overcome superior talent in raw state and alien clime, this was the time: it was a setback for the touring party. However, they were soon to fare much better.

They travelled north to Leicester, the weather remaining cheerless and wintry, but here they adapted themselves more adequately against a weaker side. The tall, fair-headed Lindsay Tuckett took nine wickets in the match, his fast-medium inswing confounding the Leicestershire batting. They managed but 128 and 121, with their skipper, professional Les Berry, batting right through the second collapse for 45. The match had turned on Alan Melville's century – the first of the English season – which included 51 in the three quarters of an hour left for play on the Saturday evening. No one else did much, and Lester had 6–42 from his leg-breaks, but it meant that the tourists had only to score 35 to win pleasingly by ten wickets.

Next, Cambridge University were overwhelmed by an innings and 153 runs. Ian Smith from Natal made his debut in England, and celebrated with a 10-wicket haul, the University hardly breaking 100 in either outing. The pitch was as perfect as a Fenner's pitch almost always was then, and the South African batsmen seized their chance. Ken Viljoen, one of the more experienced men in the party, scored 128, and a newcomer to England, Denis Begbie, made 80. The only compensation for Cambridge was the excellent fast bowling of Trevor Bailey, who took 5 for 70.

There was another big win in store at the Oval, but it had not looked anything like that at the end of the first day, for 21 wickets had fallen. On a wet wicket E. A. Watts took 5 for 31, and the South Africans slumped to a meagre 83 all out. Despite Fishlock's fortitude, Surrey could raise only 112, and once more a timely century by Melville changed the course of the game. Alec Bedser, bowling from the pavilion end after tea on the second day, toppled the South Africans with 6 for 65, only 38 being added after the interval as five wickets fell. More rain and the sufficient heat of a watery sun was enough for Surrey, and Tufty Mann, the bespectacled and courteous left-hander of Eastern Province, did the damage with 4 for 17. Considering their paltry start, a victory by a margin of 115 runs was substantial.

Rain continued to mar the South Africans' progress, and play at Southampton against Hampshire in the next fixture was heavily curtailed on the first day. Arnold hit 138 for the home side, enabling the county to declare at 300 for 6. South Africa matched this with 315, the chief contributors being George Fullerton, a tidy bat who also kept wicket, with 82, Tony Harris, the forcing Transvaal batsman, with 71, and Dudley Nourse, with his first half century of the tour. There were shocks for Hampshire in the closing hours, for as the pitch grew more responsive to spin Athol Rowan, with four wickets, was instrumental in reducing them to 79 for 7.

On 17, 19 and 20 May the South Africans faced their most crucial trial. With three good wins, as well as a loss and a draw, behind them, they played a powerful MCC XI at Lord's – and fell apart rather piteously.

After Brookes of Northamptonshire and Dodds of Essex had, in their contrasting fashions of correctitude and ebullience, given MCC a solid start, the rest of what seemed like potent batting melted before Tuckett, who took 6 for 64. But South Africa, facing only 230, barely managed half that, skittled as they were by the two young Kent players, Jack Martin and A. W. H. Mallett. MCC were able to declare at 253 for 4, Brookes getting a second half century and Denis Compton, in a portent of his greatness that season, batting freely for 97. Bruce Mitchell, who had been sadly off form, carried his bat for 103, but Sam Cook, the Gloucester spinner, finished with 6 for 44 and the tourists lost by the wide gap of 158 runs.

The temperature had remained low, the breezes stiff and the light shadowy throughout the MCC match, and poor weather haunted the visitors when they journeyed to Oxford. A freshman, W. G. Keighley of Eton, made the first century of the tour against them after the University had been put in, and Oxford moved sedately to 303 for 9. Then the South African batting produced a coherent pattern for the first time and, scoring at over 80 an hour, raced over the 500 mark. Harris, Mitchell, Melville, Nourse and Viljoen scored heavily, the last two with centuries. However, the last day's play was lost to rain, and the match was drawn. The South Africans sustained this tempo over the Whit weekend at Cardiff, where they routed Glamorgan by an innings and 131 runs. There was a most tedious day's play on the Saturday, when Bruce Mitchell pondered lugubriously over another hundred, but Rowan, with an undefeated hundred, and Mann, with 97, pressed the accelerator on Monday morning, and they declared at 479. Glamorgan did little right in the face of Tuckett and Rowan, and the game barely survived the luncheon interval on the third day.

There were still three games before the first Test: it was, compared to modern times, with its motley of one-day matches and so forth, a civilised and not too breathless induction. The Combined Services gave the South Africans little trouble at Portsmouth, only Dewes of Cambridge University and Middlesex, but presently a sailor, and the Glamorgan airman, Roberts, getting among the runs. Mitchell scored his third century in successive matches, and Plimsoll and Norman Mann were the most positive bowlers.

It was different at Lord's, where South Africa fielded a stronger side against Middlesex and forced a draw in a match not always dominated by batsmen. Mitchell gained his fourth century in a row, and Viljoen's 104, and Nourse's 92, showed the weight of the tourists' batting. In reply to their 424, Middlesex made 316 for 8 declared, but the significant event was the glowing partnership of Edrich, with 67, and Compton, with 154. The visitors made a parlous beginning to their second innings, and Sims took 6 wickets, including a hat-trick. Harris steadied the ship and, all out on 217, South Africa set the home team 326 in a little over three hours. Compton made 34, and Edrich was left undefeated with a fine 133. Although Middlesex were 100 behind at the close, the fact was not lost on Alan Melville that, with his likely Test attack in the field, Edrich and Compton had both hit timely centuries, and a reasonable second score; no other opponent had reached more than 32; only two had, in fact, managed 20 in either innings; and the Middlesex pair had tallied no less than 388 of the 532 runs recorded. It has been said that Melville, insight perhaps sharpened by worry, was the most prescient about Edrich and Compton, at the end of this game foretelling of their brilliance.

Nevertheless, he led his young team into the match with Northamptonshire in good heart and emerged with another innings victory. The Northampton pitch, normally quite accommodating, proved eccentric, and the fast bowlers Jack Plimsoll, of Western Province, and Ossie Dawson had respective match hauls of 11 and 8 wickets each. Only their last batsman, L. A. Smith, managed a half century for Northants, although Brookes grafted with typical rigour in the first innings. Northants had no fast bowler capable of making the ball shoot or rear in the awkward manner of Plimsoll and Dawson, and the South Africans batted calmly enough. Dawson, who had an excellent all-round game, Vijoen and Harris enjoyed batting in this prelude to the first Test, and with a total of 319 the South Africans won by an innings and 32 runs.

The match was over in two days, and so South Africa had a spare day before the first Test, due to begin on Saturday 7 June. Alan Melville was able to ponder his options with a little more leisure. The experienced batsmen – Mitchell, Viljoen and Nourse as well as himself – had all shown some form, but Dennis Dyer, the tall and cautious opening bat, had scarcely found his feet, so that Melville, against his earlier hopes of batting in the middle order, felt obliged to open in Dyer's stead. He was wise in his doubts. A South African weakness, now and in the past, was the central echelons of their batting. Perhaps their prevailing pattern of club cricket told against the shrewd mastery of skills honed on the long-drawn circuit of English professional cricket. Some bowlers had to learn to hold an end at the top level; some batsmen had to be able to turn an arm without embarrassment against first-class bats. Melville felt he could not play his three fastish bowlers, Tuckett, Plimsoll and Dawson, all of whom had started expeditiously. He preferred Dawson to Plimsoll, presumably on grounds of the former's batting, and also included Harris, a fine fielder, as the final batsman. Johnnie Lindsay was the pick of the wicket-keepers, but was no bat, while, ambitiously, Melville was anxious to field three spinners, Mann, Rowan and Smith. Whilst, from one angle, it was a perfectly balanced side, with all the specialities present and accounted for, it nonetheless creaked in the middle, as if swinging on a rusted hinge.

Meanwhile, the English domestic season was sedately progressing on its well-worn road to the first Test. There was the usual ballyhoo about Test hopefuls in the daily press, and naturally a watch was kept on performances against the South Africans. We shall see that these were to play, if anything, an excessive role in the selection of the England team for that opening Test.

But there was also keen interest expressed in the other matches. As the South Africans were disposing of Leicestershire in two days in the first week of May, MCC were busily conquering the might of Yorkshire, the champion county. It was a strange-looking Yorkshire side, with several pre-war stalwarts who had played a season after the war now gone, and they played a little strangely too. In wet and blustery conditions they dismissed MCC for 134, only Denis Compton, with 73, barring the path. However, the young Kent amateur, J. W. Martin, took 6 for 23, and Yorkshire were stunned to find themselves out for 81. The elegant Middlesex opener, J. D. Robertson, then drove strongly for 164, and although Yorkshire coped a trifle better in the second innings and J. V. Wilson reached 74, the champions were crushed unbecomingly by 163 runs. Those watching also noted, with surprise, that the Yorkshire fielding was inadequate – and one had to search back many years, maybe even into the last century, to find White Rose fielding as poor. It transpired that this was to be, for Yorkshire, a dark omen.

How did the counties and their most promising stars fare in that initial period? Having lost to Kent in their opening match, Derbyshire beat Worcester, conquerers of the tourists, despite the intrusion of rain, in their second fixture, Cliff Gladwin getting ten wickets in the match. Then they beat Warwickshire and, in two days and with a total of only 267, Northants by an innings. Slightly the better of a rain-affected draw at Swansea versus Glamorgan meant that Derbyshire enjoyed an excellent start, with Gladwin, of the younger players, leavening thc solid experience of a team with a distinctly '1930s' look.

Essex begun with a flurry of exciting encounters. They drew with Cambridge, and then fought out a tie with Northants. Cray's first Championship century gave Essex the early advantage, and they were left with five hours to score 240. They proceeded diligently, until spin bowling wreaked havoc, and 11 runs were required for the last wicket in twenty minutes. C. B. Clarke, the West Indian leg-spinner and one of wartime's most successful bowlers, took the last wicket with the scores level. After a solid win over Somerset, they visited Worcester, the scene of another thrilling game. Worcester raised a tall score in their first innings, but were undone by Ray Smith in their second. Tom Pearce scored 137 and 96 for Essex, but it was left to T. H. Wade, with one wicket standing, to sweep two 4s in the very last over for victory. Then there were two draws, and a defeat – but it was no discouraging beginning.

By a curio of fixture construction, Glamorgan were subjected to two heavy defeats by Yorkshire, and these were followed by the South African visit and a further loss. Rain persisted in troubling

Wales, but Glamorgan managed to organise a win over Somerset in a low-scoring affair at Newport, before lost time made a draw inevitable at Swansea against Derbyshire.

Gloucestershire drew with Oxford, and then were overwhelmed by Middlesex in a manner which gave their supporters little room for hope in any department of the sport. They rallied quickly, and inflicted huge defeats on Hampshire (an innings and 141 runs; Barnett 11 for 60 in the match) and Nottinghamshire (an innings and 167 runs; Goddard 15 for 81 in the match). Across to Taunton for a fine win at Somerset's expense, and then back to Bristol, something of a spin bowler's paradise after its treatment with sand, for Charlie Barnett's benefit. It was against Yorkshire and it was all over in two days. Sam Cook had 9 for 42 as Yorkshire toppled in the first and Tom Goddard 6 for 35 as they repeated that sorry performance in the second. Gloucester were well pleased with themselves.

Hampshire were less fortunate. Before their draw with South Africa, they had shaken Sussex by ousting them for 98, needing 185 to win, V. J. Ransom and O. W. Herman making the mischief. But then they suffered four straight defeats, to Gloucestershire, Kent, Leicester and Middlesex. A gloomy season was on the cards. Kent made a late start and played only four matches before the first Test. Of these they won three, falling only to the strong Lancashire combine. Les Ames, his wicket-keeping duties transferred to Godfrey Evans, was batting superbly. He had a century and a half-century in a 100-run win over Derbyshire; his 179 was the platform for a 9-wicket win over Hampshire; and his 82 and 58 not out put paid to Warwickshire. Kent were in fine fettle.

Lancashire, having drawn with Oxford University, won two and drew two of their first four games. Cranston had taken over the captaincy, and, in the opening Championship match against Kent at Old Trafford, he took 5 for 42 and scored 47, no mean debut and a sizeable part in an 8-wicket win. The Roses match followed at Whit weekend, and unsurprisingly it was a hard-fought draw. Lancashire's useful first-innings lead enabled them to declare, setting their opponents a target of 295. Hutton and Willie Watson emulated their century opening stand the first time round with a bigger one in the second innings – the only time, incidentally, that Yorkshire had managed this feat. Yorkshire needed 44 and had five wickets in hand when time was called. Next Lancashire confounded Sussex. After equal pickings in the first innings, Washbrook and Place (who had already scored 266 not out against Oxford) raced to 350 in less than four hours in a dazzling display, Washbrook being in particularly violent array. A large crowd gathered on the third day hoping to see Lancashire beat their long-standing first-wicket record but Cranston declared and Sussex lost by 130 runs just before the rains came. Washbrook was again in masterly form after Surrey had dismissed them cheaply and then built up a total of 435. His 251, so different in character from the previous 204 against Sussex, saved Lancashire and was Washbrook's best-ever score.

Leicestershire astonished even their most sanguine fans with an enthusiastic burst as the season opened. Certainly they lost to the South Africans in their first match, and Worcester beat them at Kidderminster in their second, but then they defeated Nottinghamshire and next Northamptonshire, each by 10 wickets, and, in between these two successes, had the better of a high-scoring draw with Essex. The spinners, Jackson and Walsh, took 19 wickets in the Nottingham match, and the latter chimed in with 11 victims in the Northants fixture, while Berry, Prentice, G. S. Watson, Tompkin and Lester were among the runs at Leicester against Essex. Only 26 wickets fell in a game which, on a firm and well-dried pitch, produced over 1,300 runs. Leicestershire were not to be denied. Hampshire came to Leicester and, on a not dissimilar wicket, were dispatched effortlessly. Walsh had another 9 wickets, and the quick bowler, Sperry, was also in evidence. Berry, consistent as ever, Watson and Riddington carried Leicester well over the 400 mark, and the home team won by an innings and 83 runs.

Middlesex began woefully, allowing Somerset the advantage in an interesting but uneven struggle, and giving little sign – an Edrich century apart – of high promise. But, like Gloucestershire, they were not downhearted, and paraded through a series of vibrant wins. Gloucestershire were, in fact, their first victims, and that, bowing briefly to the majesty of hindsight, was to have its effect on the Championship. Although Middlesex batted well enough and Robertson entertained with a fluent hundred, it was the bowlers who caught the eye. Gray and Edrich proved too pacey for the Gloucestershire batsmen, and the game was over within two days, Middlesex winning by an innings and 178 runs. Up at Birmingham, Warwickshire were beaten by an innings and 9 runs. A superb 225 from Edrich gave his county an enormous advantage; and, ably though Warwickshire tried, the spin bowling of Jack Young eventually broke them down.

Returning to Lord's, Middlesex next annihilated Worcestershire. Denis Compton, who had been peculiarly reticent in the two county matches he had figured in, now, after an early miss at the wicket, brightened a cloudy and dismal few days with two bold innings of 88 not out and his first century of the season. Edrich took 5 wickets in each innings, and Gray again bowled sharply. Rain was the only menace, but Middlesex managed to winkle out the last Worcester batsman with just twenty minutes to spare. It was a victory by no fewer than 234 runs. It took only two days to account for a struggling Sussex team, as Middlesex won by 10 wickets. Gray, Edrich and Sims were the main bowlers, as Sussex attempted to hold off the Championship leaders, but Edrich and Compton both made splendid centuries, adding 223 together. Away from the county competition, Middlesex beat Cambridge University and drew, as we have observed already, with South Africa. Compton and Edrich were assuredly ready for the Test, and many thought that one or two of their colleagues were also in stout contention.

That enthralling tie at Ilford against Essex apart, Northamptonshire were off to a woeful start. By the time of the Test they had lost three county games, all by unenviable margins, as well as having provided the South African tourists with a soft target. Dennis Brookes, often their only protector in troubled times, was not scoring heavily, and the only bright spot seemed to be the promise of their new Yorkshire wicket-keeper, Ken Fiddling. They did, however, draw with Surrey at the Oval, and had by far the best of that encounter. After Surrey's early forays through the bowling of Alf Gover, Cox, Barron and Timms all scored well to give Northants the edge, but Surrey held on grimly for the draw.

If anything, Nottinghamshire had a worse beginning to the season, and scarcely earned a Championship point. Rain ruined their first game with Worcestershire, but then they went down precipitately to Leicestershire and Gloucestershire. Next they drew with Surrey in an extremely high-scoring fixture, for by now the benignity of the Trent Bridge square was revealed in all its passive glory. June dawned as Notts gathered their first tremulous points when they scored 662 for 8 versus Essex, Keeton and Hardstaff sharing in a fluent stand of 236 and both scoring centuries. Nonetheless, they were unable to dismiss Essex twice.

Unpredictably, Somerset began with a 1-wicket victory over Middlesex. Edrich, in his first game as an amateur and presumably nursing hopes of the England captaincy, scored a fine hundred, and Somerset were tumbled out cheaply. Here it was that Maurice Tremlett made his well-nigh fictional debut – and at Lord's to boot. He followed his 3 wickets in the first innings with 5 for 39, at one time his figures reading 5 for 8. Middlesex were out for a feeble 78, leaving 176 for victory. Showing the bouyancy of the carefree club cricketer, and with one wicket remaining, Tremlett hit a 6 into the stand and then two 3s to claim the win. Just as the next hole in golf bodingly awaits to entrap the perky golfer, so are their unkind cricketing fates. Tremlett had a pair and no wickets in the next match and that signalled a disastrous run. Indeed, Somerset suffered the misery of nine consecutive defeats, many of them by yawning gaps, as their batting failed and failed again.

E. R. T. Holmes reassumed the captaincy of Surrey but the county had a hesitant beginning, drawing five county matches and their MCC fixture, and losing two games, one to the South Africans. They beat Essex in a pipe-opening friendly, and their only early Championship success was a part in Somerset's woe. Surrey won by 207 runs, most of their batsmen, including Holmes himself with a century, making some contribution, and Gover taking 12 wickets to destroy the frail Somerset batting. Alec Bedser, after the shock, even to his wholesome system, of continuous cricket through the preceding summer and winter, was not yet firing on all cylinders. Among the draws, Surrey made a tiny piece of history with their highest total ever. Unsurprisingly, it was on the placidity of a Trent Bridge strip, and they amassed 706 for 4, Fletcher, Squires, Parker and Holmes all making centuries.

Sussex, who had been wooden spoonists in 1946, began by drawing with Cambridge University, losing to Hampshire and beating Surrey in what was a sturdy and all-round team performance. This pattern of light and shade continued for, in between batterings at the hands of Middlesex and Lancashire, they satisfactorily accounted for Yorkshire at Bradford and, less astonishingly, Somerset at Taunton. In a low-scoring match, and in spite of a Hutton century, they beat Yorkshire by 3 wickets, Jack Cornford, who was bowling confidently hereabouts, having 11 victims all told on the lively northern pitch. Bold batting enabled Sussex to notch a 10-wicket victory over Somerset.

Although losing to Middlesex, Derbyshire, Yorkshire and Kent, Warwickshire found solace in three wins, each away from home, and no draws in their opening spell. A hundred from Hill and the pace of Pritchard on his debut discomfited Northants and a 9-wicket victory ensued. Somerset were the second victims, with Grove taking 7 wickets in their first and Eric Hollies 5 in their second innings. A 34-run win at Brentwood, after a tied first innings, was notable for Peter Cranmer's decision to open the Warwick second attempt with his fast bowlers, Grove and Pritchard. He feared that conditions were perilous, and he was doubtless deeply gratified when they proved him wrong with a flying start of 109.

Boosted no doubt by their win over the tourists, Worcestershire next trounced Leicestershire. This was at a rainy Kidderminster, and this victory, by 150 runs, came chiefly through the attack of Perks in the first and the spinners, Howorth and Jenkins, in the second innings. Then things turned awry. There were draws with Nottinghamshire, with Cambridge and with Surrey, but there were also defeats at the hands of Derbyshire, Middlesex and Essex.

The start of the champions' season was a little uneasy, and there was some true foretaste of Yorkshire's forthcoming travails. In the University fixtures, they beat Oxford easily but uncovered stout resistance at Fenner's, where both Willatt and Bailey scored centuries against them. Yorkshire had already lost badly to MCC, and there were to be further defeats by Sussex and Gloucestershire. Nonetheless, and as well as drawing with Lancashire, they inflicted stern beatings on Glamorgan, twice, and Warwickshire. Good hauls from Smailes and Robinson and 197 from Hutton; a Yardley century and a most balanced attack; and the destruction of

Warwickshire's first sad essay – they were out for 47 – by Bowes and Coxon: these were the features of this trio of impressive wins.

Thus did the counties begin their campaigns, logged here in alphabetic dispassion and, as the solicitors say, without prejudice. In those days too, cricket-lovers had to keep more of an eye on varsity cricket than in more modern times. At Cambridge, G. L. Willatt, that year's skipper, had set off in exemplary form, with centuries against Yorkshire and the Royal Navy, as well as 96 against Sussex, doing much to rally his troops. Cambridge had the best of two or three draws in that opening month, although they were trounced by the South Africans. Their batting was substantial, especially on those comfortable Fenner's pitches but, as so often with university cricket, the bowling was feebler. Nonetheless, Trevor Bailey was taking occasional wickets and, with his hundred against Yorkshire, he was establishing his early claim to be considered a notable all-rounder.

Oxford's batting was dominated by the gifts of M. P. Donnelly. The New Zealander scored nearly 600 runs in those first six games, four of which were drawn, while the freshman, H. A. Pawson, was also showing a promising touch. A. W. H. Mallett of Kent, opening the bowling, had already taken over 30 wickets, and was the most successful bowler at either university.

The seventeen counties and the two universities had each played six to nine games, and there had been a handful of other first-class matches, particularly those involving MCC. Thus there was no shortage of testimony as to form, as the England selectors mused over their choices for the first Test. In practice, the early batting was self-elective. Hutton had scored a massive 197 against Glamorgan and followed with further centuries against both universities and also Sussex, all at a time when Yorkshire were scrabbling a little to preserve their old authority. He also scored 95 and 86 in the Roses match. Having run into his finest form toward the end of the Australian tour, Len Hutton had then had to miss the New Zealand leg of that trip in order to return home for a throat operation. Apparently it had proceeded smoothly. His partner, Cyril Washbrook had, if more slowly, come into superb form and, in the week before the first Test, he scored two of his five post-war double centuries. The saga of Compton and Edrich was already unfolding.

Compton had scored three centuries and Edrich four, including a double century at Birmingham.

In face of this formidable quartet the several other talented early batsmen on the county circuit could only watch and wonder. Norman Yardley had inherited the captaincy from Hammond, and this also filled the all-round spot for England, while Godfrey Evans was another automatic selection – he had sprung in less than a twelvemonth to being a world-class wicket-keeper. Although Bedser, by his own taxing standards, seemed a trifle fatigued after his first-ever full season followed by a tiring tour, there was no hand raised against his choice.

Thereafter it was not so simple. England appeared to be strongest where South Africa were weakest – and vice versa. While Alan Melville fretted over opening batsmen and wicket-keeping, he was blessed with three fast bowlers. Apart from Edrich, England had no one to partner the medium to fast pace of Alec Bedser, whereas their opening four batsmen and wicket-keeper chose themselves. Perhaps a little too impressed by his early season freshness, they opted for J. W. Martin, who had bowled briskly against the tourists for MCC, but who had little other experience. Three spin bowlers were included in the twelve: Doug Wright, Eric Hollies and, once more because of recent success against the South Africans, Sam Cook of Gloucestershire. As the first two of this trio were leg-spinners, it was odds on a first cap for Cook.

This left one batting place. It was an unkindly providence which ensured that, beyond the self-selected foursome, England's most promising bats were openers, such as Jack Robertson and G. L. Willatt or even John Arnold of Hampshire and Northamptonshire's Dennis Brookes, whereas middle-order batsmen were less overt. England decided upon H. E. Dollery of Warwickshire. It was an over-cautious choice. Tom Dollery was as steady a cricketer as one might find, but his form at that point was no more than ordinary, and as he had made his debut in 1934 there was no way in which a youngster was being blooded. It was curious that the claims of Joe Hardstaff were overlooked. He had made a stunning start to the summer, with runs flowing from his handsome bat. He was a seasoned Test cricketer and if England were not prepared to introduce a third opener and disturb the established quartet, he seemed to be the better choice. That the opening Test was on his home ground in Nottingham, scene of several big scores already from Hardstaff, only added to the puzzlement. John Ikin, who had persevered so resolutely in Australia, was a little unlucky in that his leg-spin was scarcely needed, with Hollies and Wright and at a pinch Hutton available, and that Yardley took the number six berth so effectively. His nonpareil close fielding would be sadly missed.

So the two international sides were as ready as they well could be for the first Test at Trent Bridge. But there were a couple of related points beyond these preparations which might be urged. There was already an unusual, one hesitates to suggest a magical, air about the summer. After the lengthy years of war and the rather pedestrian quality of the 1946 season, the season of 1947 had started on a note of style and occasional excitement. There were huge scores and tight finishes, together with striking individual performances, many of them from established and well-loved heroes. For the many watchers and the even more plentiful perusers of the newspapers, there was something of genuine and often pleasing interest every day. The second point is that these watchers and perusers were in numerous supply. Despite the continuation of wartime restrictions and the addition of onerous peacetime regulations, cricket-lovers were out and about in their happy thousands. Demobilisation continued, and men now in their 70s recall returning home from foreign parts and spending what seems to them to have been (and perhaps was) the entire summer at Lord's or Trent Bridge or Old Trafford.

The Whit-weekend crowds at Lord's for the attractive clash of Middlesex and Sussex drew 17,000 paying customers on the Saturday and a host numbering almost 30,000 on the bank holiday Monday. Up at Old Trafford a sterling Roses contest attracted over 20,000 on each of the first two days of that same weekend. There were more than 10,000 at Bristol for the opening day of Charlie Barnett's benefit match, Gloucestershire versus Yorkshire. All the counties noted, with affectionate delight, this same quickening of interest.

It was a cyclic process. The crowds swarmed in larger numbers as the cricketers offered delicious fare, and doubtless the cricketers' adrenalin flowed as the empty stands and terraces were filled, so that in turn they strove and concentrated that much more. It had been a most entertaining opening to the season. Now for the serious passage of arms of the Test matches.

4

The Test Series

Strange that a country which has been rightly cast out from the pale of world cricket might then have been barred for a totally different reason. There had been rumours and hints that, given the grim under-productivity of the British economy, the tour could be cancelled to avoid the tug it undoubtedly might have exerted on absenteeism from vital employment. As it was, and as saner counsel realised, any such minor losses were more than compensated for by the general interest and pleasure gained from an enjoyable series. There was one other consequence of the austere economic climate, for Double British Summertime was in vogue, to the chagrin of dairy farmers and opening batsmen. It was supposed to assist in the saving of energy, but cows stuck placidly to the traditional timings and wickets proved to be unduly fresh early on. As a result, some matches began at noon.

Although the Trent Bridge square was delivering up its then customary largesse of runs, the morning of Saturday 7 June was a dismal one, and batting was arduous. There was a delay for rain; there was, thereafter, moist turf and tricky light; and the air was a trifle heavy. Winning the toss, the South Africans had felt obliged to bat, but they struggled for a couple of hours, and perhaps they were gratified by the English decision to omit Wright. Mitchell was out before lunch, and then Viljoen, having loyally grafted alongside his captain, was lbw just after the break. The score was but 44, but South Africa might easily have lost more than 2 wickets.

As it was, Dudley Nourse survived a most uncomfortable period, and, gradually, the wicket resumed its normal benign character. Melville emerged from the restraint of poor conditions to play as willowy an innings as could be wished, and Nourse, putting behind him his narrow squeaks, began to punch and smash. It was a partnership of opposites: the slim, almost frail figure of Alan Melville was one of grace and fluency; the rugged stockiness of Dudley Nourse was the base for his powerful and uncompromising hitting. Together they stayed until shortly before the close, and together they added 319 runs in impressive time. This remains South Africa's third-wicket record against England, and was, at that time, the best third-wicket stand in any Test cricket, as well as being South Africa's then best-ever wicket total. Although Melville went early on the Monday morning, Harris and Dawson added considerably to the tally, and the visitors eventually collected their largest – at that juncture – total in Test cricket: 533. With a tiny addition of 5, they were to break that record during their next trip in 1951: 538 at Leeds still stands as the record. Melville's 189 was, at that date, his country's highest individual score against England.

In truth, the last five wickets fell as only 28 runs were scrambled, in itself a reminder that South Africa were vitally reliant on a mere handful of class batsmen. Hollies and Bedser laboured strenuously to this end, but the surprise choices of Martin (1 for 111) and Cook (0 for 87) had proved untimely. The one was much too green and never fast enough; and the other, away from the more homely ranks of Gloucestershire, was vastly unsettled. It also has to be said that the English fielding, not excluding the wicket-keeping of Evans, was well below par.

Faced with this grand total, England were bundled out unceremoniously for 208, and had to follow-on. It was a matter of good all-round attacking to well-set and impeccable fields. In a minor key variation on their later, more grandiose designs, Edrich and Compton contributed 106 in the only substantial stand of the innings, and the last five batsmen managed only 9 runs between them. Tuckett had 5 for 68, and the leg-spinner, Smith, took another 3, while a cameo of note was provided by Mann: in his first Test his analysis was 0 for 10 in 20 overs, 13 of them maidens.

Before lunch on the third day, Hutton was again out cheaply, but Washbrook and Edrich both scored fifties in that tight and absorbing atmosphere. Three more wickets fell, and then Compton and Yardley joined together in a crucial partnership. In the last session of the day they added over 100 runs, a buoyant rate given the situation, but leaving England still 47 behind. Early on the final morning, and in the context of memorably alert fielding, Bruce Mitchell, regarded as one of the leading slip catchers of the age, dropped the simplest of chances from Yardley. The game probably turned on that unaccountable blunder. Compton, batting with aplomb and without error, scored 163, while Yardley was lucklessly bowled, playing across the line, one short of his maiden Test century. Several judge Compton's innings as one of his very finest, combining as it did all his cheery verve with a most judicious eye to the seriousness of the situation. The two added 237, then the highest fifth-wicket Test stand in England.

Buoyed by these stirring deeds, Godfrey Evans joined Yardley on Compton's dismissal and proceeded to maul a tiring attack. With insouciant bravura he raced to 74, and England were now establishing a small lead. There was one final scene, and that one of comedy, if not especially amusing for the South Africans. The last wicket was obdurate, so that much-needed time was used up and 51 runs added. That Martin and Hollies, both batting illiterates, should be the clowns enacting this cricketing circus act evoked a mix of relief and mirth alike from crowd and dressing-room. Had the last wicket fallen immediately, as all might have predicted, then the South Africans would have required 176 in 187 minutes, a reasonable target on a true wicket against an uneven attack. Now England had accumulated 551, and the task was the much less acceptable one of scoring 227 in 140 minutes.

Mitchell was dismissed by Bedser at once and Melville was limping, having injured a thigh, and to the disappointment of some of their supporters South Africa never seriously contemplated the chase. In the perspective of the series, perhaps they should have made the attempt. Even with a longish tail, it would have been unlikely that, had wickets fallen rapidly, the door could not have been closed. No more wickets fell; Melville, despite his damaged leg, scored his second century of the match, the first South African to accomplish that meritorious feat in Test cricket; Viljoen just reached his half century; and, at the end of the fourth day and of the game, South Africa were 166 for 1, a tantalising matter of some 60 runs away from victory. That last wicket stand had been critical.

South Africa had done so much that was right. They had endured without collapse the only difficult batting session of the game; they had swept aside the not inconsiderable might of England's batsmanship on a splendid wicket; they had amassed a record total of their own; in each and every department of the game they had been the masters. Their misfortunes had been contrary ones: in a game of long tails, they had suddenly been faced with comic unpredictability from England's last pair; and, during a matchless fielding display, a straightforward catch to rid them of Norman Yardley had been downed. Little wonder that frustrated ire mingled with genuine disappointment in the tourist camp. Even allowing for the positive character of the English fightback, there was no gainsaying that South Africa had been far the better combine and that England were fortunate to escape without defeat.

South Africa 533 (Melville 189, Nourse 149, Harris 60;
Hollies 5 for 123) and 166 for 1 (Melville 104*, Viljoen 51*)
England 208 (Compton 65, Edrich 57; Tuckett 5 for 68) and 551
(Compton 163, Yardley 99, Evans 74, Washbrook 59, Edrich 50;
Smith 4 for 143)
Match drawn

That draw, the consequence of rather good luck and a modicum of good management, had great, if negative, effect on the symbolism of 1947 as a cricket season. In those four days the reality and the myth of the glories of 1947 came close to being stillborn. The fond memory is of England pulverising the South Africans, and the truth, while not as simplistic nor as absolute as that, is not too separate from the memory. A South African win might have changed the whole tenor of the series and led to different processes and outcomes; at the very least, and had nothing else changed, the rubber would have looked rather different arithmetically. Some of these aspects are intangibles. The second Test was only nine days away. The teams dispersed exuding annoyance and relief, not, as it might have been, bliss and gloom; that was a critical distinction.

The South Africans spent the intervening weekend relieving their frustrations on a weak and demoralised Somerset team at Taunton. Plimsoll and Dawson, emphasising the depth of South Africa's fast-medium attack, took 15 wickets between them as Somerset crashed twice. Mitchell, Begbie, Nourse and Viljoen scored half centuries to ensure a victory by an innings and 43 runs, despite the loss of almost the whole of Saturday to rain.

Both establishments had been deep in thought. The South Africans, while confident, must have noted with distaste the simmering form of England's batsmen, and it was obvious that, during the second Test, the field placing was careful and personalised. There was no need to ponder over team selection: the XI that had served the tourist cause so competently at Trent Bridge was listed for Lord's.

It was the England selectors who had longer pause for thought. Martin and Cook were abruptly dropped, and neither played Test cricket again. Their careers took very differing turns. The amateur fast bowler had a brief and sporadic career: he played only seven first-class games in 1947, including only two county matches, and he had faded from the scene in a year or so, with only 129 wickets in all. The professional slow bowler played until 1964, and enjoyed the combined standing of effective performer and jocose character which has often been a blessing on the county circuit as he worked towards his 1,782 wickets. They were replaced by D. V. P. Wright, who had spent his time rubbing the noses of the selectors in the dirt with 11 wickets for Kent against Northamptonshire, and the reliable Derbyshire bowler, George Pope. Hollies was retained, but as the only left-hander, Denis Compton, bowled chinamen, there was some variety, and no one could deny that England's best two spin bowlers were on show. Edrich was destined to open the bowling with Bedser, and – a final change – Charlie Barnett was chosen as the fifth batsman instead of Tom Dollery.

It certainly looked a more experienced side, even if the tail was none too solid. Hollies, who had shared with Martin in that popular last-wicket stand at Nottingham, finished his Warwickshire career with runs well behind wickets: 1,544 runs against 2,201 wickets. Dollery was unlucky not to be allowed a second bite at the South African cherry, but his 9 and 17 at Trent Bridge had not been impressive.

Golden summer had still not broken. There was rain in the air on Saturday 21 June in London, and in fact there was a brief stoppage for the weather. Nonetheless, the pleasure of an international match in the capital was not to be denied, and the South Africans, through their sterling efforts at Nottingham, made for attractive guests. Over 30,000 were packed into the ground well before the start; the gates were then closed on crowds estimated to be several thousand strong. It all created a stirring air of expectation.

England won what was to prove to be a valuable toss, and started extremely slowly. Hutton was a little out of sorts, and the energetic Tuckett made his in-swingers fizz off the damp turf. It took until after lunch to notch 75 runs. Still, it was solid enough, and Washbrook scored a sound 65, Tuckett juggling mesmerically with the ball to catch him in the slips.

This brought Edrich and Compton together at 96 for 2 midway through the afternoon session. By tea 111 runs had been added; by the close, despite a half hour break for rain, it was 312 for 2. Despite bowling of general efficiency, despite fielding, including the wicket-keeping of Johnnie Lindsay, that never for a moment lapsed from a high degree of keenness, the visitors were subjected to imperious assault.

It was after lunch on the second day before Edrich was bowled. The stand had been worth 370, and that remains England's biggest third-wicket stand in all Test cricket. Edrich, favouring the pulled drive and, in general, the on-side, made 189; while Compton, dexterous in placement through the covers and mid-wicket, scored 208, his first double century in Tests. There had appeared to be little or no anxiety in the batting, and that mood of gaiety, especially in the case of Denis Compton, conveyed itself to a hugely satisfied crowd. Primed by the activities of Saturday, the Monday gathering once more topped 30,000.

The dominance of the Middlesex pair was underlined by following events. It is true that Yardley requested fast scoring, and Barnett crashed about him for a militant 33. Nonetheless, the England innings subsided dramatically after Compton's departure at 515. Tuckett had Compton caught by Rowan, and then took 4 more wickets, that is, 5 for 20 in his last spell before England declared. The score was 554 for 8 – the highest in England against these opponents – and certainly something like 100 runs had been savaged in an hour after lunch. But that was still an undesirable tumbling of wickets, and South African supporters must mentally have subtracted 397 – the Middlesex contribution –

from 554 and found the 157 proffered by the remainder a trifle galling.

There was no downheartedness about the South African response; no flurry of quick wickets as sometimes maims a side which has suffered drudgery in the field. Bruce Mitchell, wary and loath to commit himself, gave much more substantial aid to the ever-polished Melville than he had at Nottingham, and 95 were added in reasonable time. It required a quicksilver stumping by Evans off Compton (England's sixth bowler) to be rid of Mitchell, and then Viljoen was bemused totally by Wright. Early on the third day Melville completed his third successive Test century, and, as he had made 103 in the second innings of the last Test at Durban in 1939, this gave him four consecutive hundreds against England. He obtained expected support of the most resilient kind from Dudley Nourse, who scored 61, but when these two stalwarts were dismissed and although Dawson and Harris, as at Trent Bridge, hit about with some abandonment, the innings fell away. Its early resolution was replaced by sorry ineptitude. Wright spun his leg-breaks and googlies at disconcerting velocity, and from a one-time 290 for 4, South Africa found themselves disconsolate and baffled, 327 all out.

It was now the afternoon of the third day, and as if transfigured by the conventional royal visit and presentation at that time in the Lord's Test, Edrich flung himself into the attack with furious zeal. Melville and Viljoen heard their stumps fly behind them, and it was left to Nourse and Mitchell to restore order and sanity to that Tuesday evening. Needing 227 to avert an innings defeat, South Africa were 120 for 2 at the close, and not looking too uncomfortable. Edrich struck again with the very first ball of the last day, clean bowling Nourse, his third victim in that same uncompromising fashion. That was a lethal blow, and, although Mitchell and Dawson hammered out 70 or so runs, things now looked bleak for South Africa. Edrich could not be kept unoccupied, catching both those batsmen brilliantly in the slips – and taking another to end the innings. Once more Wright was the avenger. Having persuaded Mitchell to edge that catch to Edrich, he again wiped out the bedraggled tail. Just before Mitchell was fourth out, the score was 192 – and only a paltry 60 runs were added as those

7 wickets fell. Wright had another 5 wickets, giving him match figures of 10 for 175.

South Africa had edged marginally in front, and it was left to Hutton and Washbrook solemnly to strike the 26 runs needed for a 10-wicket win. Several commentators pointed to the fact that the last day had created a similar position to the final day at Nottingham, albeit with reversed roles. It has to be said that England did not make the same heavy weather of that situation as the unlucky South Africans had done, for Wright had guaranteed that there would be no last-ditch heroics.

It had been a splendid game of cricket. Great crowds had witnessed pleasurable performances, with only a drab display by South Africa's lower order batsmen standing between them and an honourable draw. A 10-wicket gulf was a little unjust, when one remembered the hard-working bowlers, the application of the earlier batsmen and, above all, the excellence of the fielding. On their side, the English bowling was still curiously unbalanced, and the fielding was, at times, woeful. Half a dozen chances were missed, four of them off the perspiring and doubtless peeved Bedser. It was a two-man band. Apart from getting three-quarters of the runs, Edrich and Compton had taken 7 wickets between them, all, incidentally, mainline batters. Edrich had also pocketed 4 catches. England were strangely uncoordinated.

England 554 for 8 dec. (Compton 208, Edrich 189, Washbrook 65; Tuckett 5 for 115) and 26 for 0 dec.
South Africa 327 (Melville 117, Nourse 61; Wright 5 for 95) and 252 (Mitchell 80, Nourse 58; Wright 5 for 80)
England won by 10 wickets

There was barely more than a week before the third Test, and the South Africans fielded their second string players in the two intervening fixtures. The first was a drawn match at Trent Bridge, where both sides batted well, scoring over 300 apiece, and left little time for a second innings. Keeton scored 90 for Nottinghamshire, but Hardstaff was not on his best form. After Mitchell had scored 97 for South Africa, it was a spirited last-wicket stand from Mann and Plimsoll which gave them first innings lead.

Plimsoll, with his accurate left-arm bowling, then proved too much for Northumberland. His 11 wickets and Viljoen's 130 gave their side an innings victory up at Newcastle. J. H. G. Deighton was the only Northumbrian batsman of substance. The fixture itself may sound curious in today's connotation, but to the credit of tourists and tour organisers in those days, a minor county, especially one enjoying some success, might occasionally be included in the itinerary. It ensured that a good grade of cricket was featured in places not conventionally associated with the first-class game.

It was now July, but the weather had not yet reached the sun-drenched glories recalled by all cricket-lovers around in 1947. The third Test was at Old Trafford, and wind and rain were both heavy. Bails and once even a sightscreen were dislodged, and playing cricket was a thoroughly uncomfortable business. Kenneth Cranston and Cliff Gladwin were brought into the England team, Bedser and Pope being stood down. Neither had done well in the preceding Test, but in Bedser's case the selectors were civilised enough to write explaining their decision, insisting it was a matter of resting a fatigued bowler of whose quality they were genuinely assured.

Cranston's inclusion was a cavalier choice. Although he had become well-known in wartime cricket and had a considerable reputation as a Liverpool Competition club cricketer, he had played only thirteen first-class matches, that is, the sum total of the Lancashire fixtures since he had been made captain. There was no doubting that he was a naturally gifted all-rounder, and the taciturn Lancashire coach, Harry Makepeace, had been heard to declare that Cranston had been the most talented young man to come under his tutelage. It was also true that England required some all-round stiffening, in the field as well as with bat and ball, but it was still a gamble. Cranston was a very inexperienced cricketer. Such could not be said of Gladwin, for he was fast becoming the latest in a long series of Derbyshire fast-medium bowlers, naggingly tight and indomitably tireless. Jack Robertson was also in the twelve, but it was no more than a courtesy call. It marked his worth in the order of things, but he may have found that token of esteem inconvenient.

He missed a county match, and there was never really a chance he would have been picked.

South Africa made a change or two. After his 7 wickets in the Trent Bridge Test, the leg-spinner, Smith, had suffered a little at Lord's and was a rabbit among batsmen. Plimsoll was taking wickets regularly, and while, in those innocent times, three medium-pacers appeared excessive, his claim could not be ignored. Harris was a trifle unlucky to go, following his 60 at Trent Bridge and a useful 30 at Lords, but the South Africans were eager to bolster the early batting. They obviously felt it keenly that they seemed just to have four Test batsmen, and of course it had been hoped that Dyer would open the batting. His patient 62 against Nottinghamshire was enough to persuade Melville and his advisers that the time was ripe for that experiment. On paper, both sides looked better balanced.

Alan Melville won the toss, and chose to bat in chilled, damp and blustery conditions. It was a noon start, and in fact the pitch was to prove less difficult on that Saturday than later. Overall, it was a neutral, self-cancelling kind of day. England had no bowler of the velocity and height to take advantage of the lively wickets which were then a feature of Old Trafford, whilst Wright was badly incommoded by a poisoned foot. Everyone bowled adequately, and all seven bowlers were tried, but it was all rather humdrum. For their part, the tourists lacked the courage or invention to snatch the initiative, and their innings was, like the Wandering Minstrel, 'a thing of shreds and patches'. Slowly they assembled 339, no mean score, and one that should have ensured them victory. But it was very low-key.

The debutant Dyer defended strictly for his 62, but Melville went early, and after an enterprising start Nourse gave Cranston his first Test wicket. Mitchell batted well, but was run out needlessly for 80, and Viljoen, despite injury, battled to 93. Although the remaining batsmen took some digging out, they contributed negligibly as far as runs were concerned, and at the last the South Africans were to find themselves short of 70 or 80 runs.

Sunday night had brought severe rainfall, and when England batted after Monday lunchtime the continuing wind and the newfound sun created some distress. Washbrook and Hutton were soon out, and now Compton and Edrich made probably their greatest stand of the summer. Against rearing pace and accurately turned spin, they throve and matured. Initially, as Edrich grimly defended, the fluent genius and buoyant disposition of Compton ran amok. Playing late and potently with the often spiteful turn, he had the adroit control and power to seize command and score a matchless century in less than two and a half hours. After tea Edrich greeted the new ball with a volley of scorching shots and, batting on through the delays of the rainy third day, he made a most admirable 191. Yardley, Cranston and Evans chipped in with minor acts of aggression, and, against rational expectation, England had 478 and a healthy lead. Tuckett had 4 and Plimsoll 3 wickets.

The fourth and last day, in fiercesome conditions, was dominated by Dudley Nourse, who was destined to play the major innings of his career, and one that merited a less disappointing finale. With staunch assistance from his captain and from the injured Viljoen, he essayed that alliance of forbearance and belligerence that must be the true mark of excellence in dire circumstances. It was his refusal to become cramped by slow and medium pace on a pitch of variable bounce and his nerveless readiness to strike lethal blows that characterised his 115. Some critics rated the innings as brilliant as any played in that star-studded season.

It should have been enough to permit South Africa survival, if not better. As if distressingly to underpin his exceptional show of daring, the visitors' innings subsided pitifully. The fourth wicket did not fall until the score was 217: they were all out for 267.

It detracts not from the performance of Nourse to complain about the inadequacy of the English attack. With Wright not yet fully fit, it was left once more to Edrich – on a spinner's wicket – to take the honours. Out of sheer zest he found the thrust to capture 8 wickets in the match, several of them good ones, including the yorking of the indefatigable Nourse to end his imperious knock. It was unfair to expect Compton to be expert enough to play the role of frontline spin bowler – and so there were the England XI, with a pitch tailor-made for orthodox slow bowling, and yet without either a left-arm leg-break or a right-arm off-break bowler.

Some 150 minutes remained, and the home side needed 129, perhaps a more difficult task than it seems at first sight, given the awkwardness of the pitch. Certainly there were several veteran spin bowlers on the county scene who would have relished the challenge. Athol Rowan should have been in his element, but his off-spin was untypically lacking conviction, drifting uneasily between attack and defence, and he bowled four overs only. That in itself was mysterious, and maybe there were other factors, possibly a disagreement with the captain, to explain so brief an intercession. The always accurate Mann demonstrated what might have been, turning the ball vindictively and ousting Hutton and Compton without ceremony. The wily Washbrook, ever the acute tactician and knowledgeable in the frets and fancies of his Lancastrian heath, hit out quickly, as he had done in the first innings, desirous of easier runs before the effect of the roller vanished. His speedy 40 was a solid help-meet, and then it was aptly left to Edrich, who had been on the field of play for almost the duration of the match, to guarantee an England win by 7 wickets.

It had been a game which had matched the majesty of some individual batting – Edrich, Compton, Nourse – against indifferent bowling on a devilish track of genuine problem. John Arlott concluded that it would be remembered 'as the most disastrously wasted opportunity for bowlers in any Test'. In spite of the dispiriting climatic variations, sizeable crowds had gathered, and it had been another interesting encounter. The South Africans again must have kicked themselves for letting slip a welcoming chance of victory. They could, of course, point to personal lapses, just as, no doubt, they must have brooded dolefully over the vengeance that Compton and Edrich visited upon them. In real terms, the want of 100 runs over both innings made the difference between losing and assuredly saving the game, or even, just possibly, winning it.

South Africa 339 (Viljoen 93, Mitchell 80, Dyer 62) and 267 (Nourse 115, Melville 59)
England 478 (Edrich 191, Compton 115) and 130 for 3
England won by 7 wickets

South Africa retreated to Ireland to play a couple of minor and relaxing games. They flew from Manchester's Ringway airport direct to Dublin, and found the same meteorological shades in attendance. The Trinity College ground was under water, and play was ruled out for the first of the scheduled two days. Although seven other bowlers were utilised, Rowan was given a lengthy spell against the Gentlemen of Ireland. He ended with 9 for 39. The South Africans nonchalantly batted out the remainder of the day, and then travelled north to Belfast. Here, and on a pitch affected by rain, they demolished the Gentlemen of Ireland in one day. They won by an innings and 125 runs, the Irishmen mustering only 93 in both attempts. Rowan, obviously in an effort to boost his flagging confidence, bowled unchanged and took a further 12 wickets. The generous-hearted South Africans cheerfully agreed to stay over the weekend and participate in a one-day game. The Irish off-spinner, J. C. Boucher took 7 wickets, and Ireland were delighted to win by 6 wickets.

It was time for sterner stuff, and this took the hardy shape of a mini northern tour before the fourth Test at Leeds. Rain interfered dreadfully with play at Derby, and it was early on the last day –the first ball of the morning, to be precise – before both first innings were completed, the South Africans lagging by 52. In that storm-laden and dank atmosphere, Derbyshire were, however, dismissed for 32. Their destroyer was Ian Smith. In a feat unequalled in English first-class cricket, he took 6 for 1 in 4.5 overs, including the hat-trick. His match figures were 13 for 66. Derbyshire advanced by only 2 meagre runs as their last 7 wickets fell. George Pope, who took 10 wickets in the match, caused difficulties, but the tourists persevered, and won by 3 wickets – and there was still over half an hour until tea.

Sheffield was the next venue, and as ever in those decades Yorkshire were the prime opponents, the national team apart. With plentiful rain on the second day and obdurate batting from both camps, a draw was soon inevitable. George Fullerton followed up useful contributions at Derby with two more valuable innings, and he kept wicket tidily; this was of interest to the South African management. Of more emotional concern to the Yorkshire crowd was the fate of Len Hutton, doubtful for Leeds because of sickness. He scored 89 before lunch on the second day, and went on to score a most satisfying century. All looked well for the Test.

South Africa completed their wanderings with a trip to Paisley and a two-day drawn match with Scotland. Rain still persisted and curtailed play. A young minister, Aitchison, pleased with a century, something of a rarity in such games, but Fullerton consolidated his pressure for a Test place with a hard-hitting 129.

Ovenstone, one of three wicket-keepers in the party, had broken a finger in June in the Nottingham match and, able although Lindsay was, it was the later South African batting that was causing anxiety. Thus Fullerton was introduced into the Test side, and the unfortunate Lindsay stepped down. Nor could Smith's claim be overlooked, and Plimsoll, perhaps in part because of Edrich's cruel assault on him at Old Trafford, lost his place.

England also made two changes. Their search for an opening bowler continued. Martin, Pope and Gladwin had been tried and found wanting, while Edrich was far away the most successful of the quicker bowlers. Harold Butler, whose luckless fate it was to batter away on the unfeeling square at Trent Bridge, was asked to play, and it was certain that, at least, he would extract life from a pitch, if life there was. The luxury of two leg-break bowlers was now seen as an extravagance and Hollies was left out. In came Jack Young, the Middlesex left-hander, as England determined that an uncomplicated finger-spinner was a necessity.

Headingly was full on the first day, Saturday 26 July. The Friday night had seen heavy rain, and the crowd of 31,000 sat through a day of leaden skies and sober light. The outfield was very damp, and the square itself was wet, so much so that the pitch was unresponsive and sluggish. It was obviously unpleasant for batting, but on balance, bowling and fielding were more arduous chores. As it was, South Africa made poor use of the situation after winning the toss. They were completely undermined by the abrupt loss of Melville for a duck, and recovery seemed beyond them. Their defensive response was over-wary, with barely double figures in the first hour. When the new ball was taken after 55 overs they were only 85 for 2. The sole stand of numerical note was that between Mitchell and Nourse, both of whom laboured over patient 50s, and by six o'clock and with not yet a hundred overs bowled, the South Africans were all out for 175.

On this occasion England's opponents could curse only themselves and not the fates. The bowling had been tidy enough, but not demanding, while the fielding, if improved, was not unblemished.

Butler, in his first Test, watched in chagrin as a couple of slip chances went begging. Nonetheless, he was the pick of the bowlers, having 4 victims, with Edrich, inevitably, taking a further 3. Norman Yardley had had the sense to harry timid batsmen with close fields and frequent bowling changes. He deployed six bowlers in all, despite the brevity of the proceedings – and the South Africans, for all their natural ability and seeming confidence, had found no sense of resolve and purpose.

Play, having begun at midday, continued until seven o'clock, and in still murky light (both captains were asked not to overdo the pace from the grandstand end, where there was no sightscreen) Hutton and Washbrook securely played out the remaining hour.

Len Hutton, although capped in 1937, was, by reason of oddities of fixtures and the inconveniences of war, appearing for England on his native soil for the first time. Well set as he was over the weekend, there was a natural hunger among his fellow Yorkshiremen to relish the Monday morning. They arrived in their many thousands, and with 35,000 on the ground, the gates were locked, and thousands more were turned away in bitter frustration. The heavens opened upon them and a major thunderstorm took place. The ground was temporarily flooded, and there was little shelter for those on the terraces, who were determined to guard jealously the perch that long queueing had earned. Others, many, many hundreds of others, were worse off, having to sit, once the match began an hour late, on sodden grass. It was then the practice, before the advent of all-numbered seats and of measured boundaries, to steal a circle of the sward to accommodate spectators when crowds were large. This, incidentally, meant that, on less popular days of the same match, batsmen were displeased to see the boundary retreating to the rails. In this Test, and it was an occasional happening elsewhere, play was held up when excited crowds spilled over the provisional boundary line. But this was purely the result of overcrowding – there might have been a depth of ten or a dozen spectators on the grass at some points – and discomfort; there was no misconduct, and almost all spectators tried to behave civilly.

At least, on this occasion, the story had a happy ending. Len Hutton scored a century. Sitting in a cramped lump of humanity on damp seats or soaking turf, with the thundery air intolerably oppressive, patience garnered, for once, its just reward. Hutton had had an undistinguished series, and there must have been many Yorkshiremen who found the heady yarns of the Compton/Edrich magicianship galling as their own hero stumbled to 17, 9, 18, 13 not out, 12 and 24. Two other elements added to the all but fictional ethos. There was Hutton's near missing the game because of illness, and there was the effect of the thunderstorm. This produced conditions ideal for spin bowling, and yet the humidity, especially on a drying wicket, also offering help to swing bowling. The South Africans should have harassed England mightily.

That they did not was primarily due to a stand of high technical acumen by Hutton and his partner, Washbrook. An early escape apart, Washbrook joined Hutton in an exposition of expertise and the accumulation of 141 runs. They concentrated on deadening the spin but without ever missing the opportunity to place shorter deliveries through the field for valuable runs. While not as thrilling and vivid as some of the stands negotiated by their Middlesex colleagues, this demonstration was, in the circumstances both of the physical conditions and the match itself, not surpassed by them. Washbrook, after surviving a couple more chances, was out for 75, but Hutton continued, faultlessly, to exactly 100, to the massive acclaim of the crowd. Then he slipped and was run out. Compton, Edrich and Yardley made grafting contributions, but each found it difficult to capitalise on that excellent start, itself a statement of the achievement of the two senior northern professionals. Mann took 4 wickets, while Rowan, after an uneasy start, appeared to gain in assurance but bowled tightly rather than threateningly.

Although they were only 7 wickets down and 142 runs ahead, Yardley, always a captain of intelligence and shrewdness, declared. The South Africans, psychologically buffeted, found themselves batting again at first light on the third day. Edrich performed his customary breakthrough and Young took his first Test wicket, so that, although the pitch was not anywhere as difficult as perhaps Yardley had hoped, the South Africans were groping and uncoordinated. Melville and Nourse tried to restore some credence, but Compton, with a catch at short extra-cover which tested belief, ended the former's effort, and Butler had the latter lbw. Nourse did, however, assemble his second 50 of the game.

The others struggled on, making 10s and 20s, but no one else appeared capable of heavy scoring. The end of the innings was dramatic. Cranston, who had played an undistinguished part in both his Test matches, began his seventh over. It was destined for the history books. He dismissed batsmen with the first, third, fifth and sixth deliveries, one of the most amazing overs in Test history. As well as bordering on the legendary, it exposed the frailty of the lower order of South Africa's batting in the cruellest manner.

They had only managed to create a margin of 42 runs, and with methodical soundness the England openers made sure of the rubber, Hutton sweeping Mann for 6 with time in hand on the late Tuesday afternoon.

That 10-wicket victory was resounding, if not enthralling. In three days England, while suffering the worst of the conditions, contrived to trounce the South Africans. There were none of the excuses or explanations of the other games; and there could certainly be no pretence that there had been, as in those other Tests, junctures where with a little better fortune another result might have been possible. Mann had tried his best, with 4 good first-innings wickets, and Mitchell and Nourse had batted reasonably well. Aside from these minor attainments, it was all dross. The bowling had lacked penetration at the crucial time, and that feeble tail could brag of only a distressing consistency – in each innings, the last 7 wickets had fallen while exactly 54 runs had been added. Possibly the simplest rationalisation was that the English players were superior in what had been non-South African conditions. On the brighter side, and with only three days' play, the Headingley Test had still proved bountiful: gate receipts of £16,000 were a record for Leeds, and something of a tribute to the tourists' popularity.

South Africa 175 (Mitchell 53, Nourse 51) and 184 (Nourse 57)
England 317 for 7 dec. (Hutton 100, Washbrook 75) and 47 for 0
England won by 10 wickets

The touring party had three days' grace before their next fixture. This was a traditional encounter with Glamorgan over the bank holiday weekend, and South Africa won by 40 runs. It was a most interesting battle. The rain had continued to stream, and the Swansea wicket was much affected by this. Harris played easily his best innings of the tour, and his hundred made the difference, for Alan Watkins of Glamorgan was the only other player to rise above 40 in the match. Spin bowling dominated: the veteran John Clay had match figures of 11 for 162, and Rowan 10 for 145.

The thundery storms of the last few days were subsiding, and at long last the cloudless warmth of summer emerged. It appeared to liberate the South Africans. They next mauled Warwickshire without let or mercy. They scored over 500 in reply to Warwickshire's hard-won total of 330, and as well as a hundred from Ken Viljoen, Dudley Nourse hit a powerful 205, the best individual score of the tour. Tuckett and Dawson then removed Warwickshire for 76 on the last morning to complete a huge innings victory: at one point, the home team were 11 for 5.

There was a longer gap between the fourth and fifth Tests, and as the climate brightened the South Africans were eager to make use of the time. Washbrook held the Lancashire batting together with a century at Manchester, and Bruce Mitchell replied in kind with 131. Cranston took 5 wickets for Lancashire, and the South Africans had to be content with a draw. Dropped chances marred the South African performance. They then encouraged themselves with a clearcut win over the strong Gloucestershire XI at Cheltenham. With steady, rather than enterprising, batting, they constructed a solid position, and 11 more wickets for Rowan were sufficient for them to register a win by 133 runs.

They travelled to London on the Friday evening after that heartening performance, ready to face England for the fifth time. The Oval, as usual, was the venue, and it was Saturday 16 August.

The South Africans stayed with a losing side. Perhaps Plimsoll and Lindsay and possibly Harris were the unlucky ones, but on the whole the management probably believed that this was their best combine, come what may. As the games with the counties testified, it was an effective one, but one just a shade short of that spread of coherent talent that creates an efficient international team.

England were forced by injuries to reconstruct their side. The loss of Edrich with a damaged shoulder was troublesome, for he was both number three batsman and opening bowler. His Middlesex team-mate, Jack Robertson, was almost an automatic replacement, and Bill Copson of Derbyshire, a little elderly now for such activities but genuinely quick, was also introduced. Harold Butler was very unlucky. A success at Leeds with match figures of 7 for 66, he pulled a muscle and just failed to be restored to fitness. Copson's Derbyshire partner, Cliff Gladwin, was recalled, Alec Bedser being left on fallow ground for the rest of the series. Charlie Barnett was the batsman who had to retire, and, in all charity, he had done little outstanding, with only 63 runs in his four attempts and thirteen fruitless overs. Some would have preferred Robertson to have enjoyed an earlier chance; each opened the batting for his county, so that a switch of either to the centre of the order was much the same approach. Dick Howorth of Worcestershire, like Copson aged 38, replaced Jack Young. The clash of this Test with the critical Middlesex and Gloucestershire fixture may, with the rubber decided, have had a bearing on this decision. Having, so to say, replaced Barnett with Robertson and with Edrich injured, it might have looked severe to rob Middlesex also of their important spin bowler. However, with the tail lengthening a little with the advent of the Derbyshire bowlers, the fact that Howorth was, as he proved, a dependable all-rounder was possibly the selectors' more realistic and less sentimental assessment.

The heatwave had been intense, so much so that, in spite of the heavy rains of June and July, a fortnight's scorching sunshine had parched the outfield a sort of yellowy-grey pigmentation. The wicket was slow and subject to turn, albeit at dilatory pace, and inevitably it wore dustily. The daily use of the roller kept it decently bound and unified, and it was at the end of each day when it caused most anxiety. For both players and spectators the game was played in the sultriest of conditions, with the temperature unvarying in its sometimes unbearable heat.

The game began defensively. Melville set cautious fields; Hutton and Washbrook refused to contemplate risk. Fielders were placed to prevent boundaries, and the dry outfield ensured the ball sped to them so rapidly that only singles resulted. If anything, the pressure was on South Africa: their strategy seemed tentative, whereas the English response was untroubled. The day wore on. Hutton consolidated his recent improved international form with a flawless and unhurried 83, while everyone else, bar the luckless Robertson, stayed long enough to add rational support. Compton and Yardley scored 50s and Cranston and Evans scored 40s. Having conspired to run out Evans, Cliff Gladwin contrived to assemble a roughshod and unlikely half-century, so that the later order was more fruitful than expected. Only Copson and Robertson of the eleven failed to make double figures, and although by the more stimulating criteria of the era the rate was slow, England's 427 established a position of strength.

Tufty Mann maintained his meticulous accuracy during these long and torrid hours. He took 4 wickets, but the other bowlers looked a little jaded and hesitant. It is worthy of comment that, over an innings that endured through almost eight hours, 190 overs were bowled, an average of nearly 24 an hour. The great crowds, perched and squatted perspiringly in the oppressive sun, had more actual cricket to watch than their counterparts today.

South Africa again opened, as they had always wished to do, with Dyer, hopeful that his recent 74 against Gloucestershire would bolster his morale. It was not to be. He failed once more; Viljoen could not master Wright, who had tormented him throughout the season; and Nourse fell to Howorth's first ball in Test cricket, thus placing the left-hander in the most select of coteries, of whom Maurice Tate must be the most famous member. The South Africans had no taste for historical curio; they were 78 for 3, and the long tail listlessly awaited.

Bruce Mitchell set himself to mend these tumbling fences. In rocklike certitude, and with some of the immobility of stone, he laboured for the cause – and yet when a delivery was punishable it was booked as one of his fourteen imperious boundaries. Melville, as always, appearing to be in tranquil command, and Dawson, more assured than in previous Tests, were his leading allies. Howorth matched Mann for steadiness, taking 3 wickets, but Mitchell's six-hour vigil and formidable century rescued the tourists from the ignominy of following on. And, sure enough, fifteen minutes after his dismissal by Copson, the innings was ended, the last 3 wickets adding but 9 runs. Copson took the new ball, was cut by Mitchell for 4, and then captured the last 3 wickets in a seven-over spell without another run being taken off him.

It was around midday on Tuesday, the third day, when England resumed 125 ahead. Hutton and Washbrook once more ensured there was a no-nonsense start, and, this time, it was lively as well. Robertson managed 30, without doing justice to his well-merited repute for aplomb, but in the event Compton was the cynosure for all eyes, so that his partners' unassertiveness was less noticed. Denis Compton, druidic in his worship of the sun, revelled in the sweaty conditions, which often were near intolerable for other cricketers, including some of the South Africans. Liberated, versatile, hugely entertaining, Compton answered his skipper's call for quick results with exaggerated devotion. In less than two hours he marshalled 113 out of the 178 scored. It was a show of extempore batting, dazzling and little short of insolence. It must be remembered that other wickets fell, so that his excessive forcing of the pace was a calculated risk. England were 180 for 5 at one stage, and a sudden collapse then, in the context of the game, might have led to difficulties.

After his departure, Howorth and Evans smote cheerily and expansively, so that England were able to declare at 325 for 6. The whole business had taken only three and a half hours, approaching a run-rate of 100 an hour, and the rattled visitors had half an hour left to bat. Rowan took 3 wickets, as he had done in the first innings, but in general the bowling had been savaged.

A total of 450 was needed, but the pitch turned out to be at its best on the last day, and South Africa, with three or four world-class batsmen, faced a side weak in high pace. The sad figure of Dyer, lbw to Wright, having already been dropped in the slips, trudged back into the pavilion right at the close of those last thirty almost runless minutes, so that in effect South Africa had the whole of Wednesday to score the runs, with 9 wickets in hand.

The South African plan soon became apparent. Mitchell's job was to withstand the siege faithfully, while others essayed skirmishing attack, as the tourists tried to score the 70 or so an hour required. The first part of the schedule was an unparalleled success, for, monumentally, Mitchell was not out at the close, having emulated Melville's two hundreds at Trent Bridge, and having been in attendance on the field for all but fifteen minutes of the four extremely tiring and sticky days. It was a memorial to patience and loyalty. Viljoen scampered 30 or so quick runs, and then Nourse demonstrated the most aggressive intent. His awesome hitting earned him 97 swift runs, and in mid-afternoon the total was 232 for 2.

South Africa had every chance of victory. Nourse was then out to a peculiar ball from Howorth – there were fanciful cries for lbw and caught behind, but the square-leg umpire had noted the ball dislodge the leg bail, and Nourse was bowled. The next forty-five minutes saw the decline of the South African cause. Melville, on whom so much depended, failed, whilst Dawson and Fullerton, both attacking players, did not last long. Of a sudden, South Africa had only 4 wickets left, and over two hours to survive. In three quarters of an hour they had switched from likely winners to probable losers. It was about this time that the brooding and prudent Mitchell reached his century, and, although he had advanced his tempo as Nourse had looked sure and powerful, it had been a lethargic progression – for instance, he had scored only 36 in the two and a half hours before lunch.

Nonetheless, he was still present. Mann accompanied Mitchell's act of methodical defiance for some little while, and then Tuckett, who many thought had been overbowled and overstrained on the tour and who must have been a much fatigued cricketer, saved the deteriorating reputation of the South African tail with a whole-hearted 40 not out. Mitchell finished with a massive 189 not out. Apart from a dropped catch by Evans late on in this dour performance, it was technically faultless.

At the end of a day of changing fortunes, South Africa were 423 for 7, just 28 runs behind. Of course England had had the advantage of being able to press with attacking fields, without bothering too much about the runs, which also came a trifle cheaply in the last half hour. However, it was to England's severe discredit that they were unable to remove the remaining South Africans, and that disappointingly they had taken only 1 wicket, from amongst a notoriously fragile lower order, in the last two and more hours of play. For their part, the South Africans, even allowing for the tactical factors – Yardley might, in trouble, have tightened the stranglehold, had defeat looked imminent – must also have been downhearted. Apart from the unseemly collapse of their middle-order batsmen, they must have wondered whether more freedom before lunch might have been more propitious. That said, there was no one who could really muster the gall to criticise Mitchell, the St Peter, as it were, of the South African establishment.

It had been an interesting game, and its fluctuations and pulsations had been enjoyed by multitudes. Nearly 80,000 had attended, and £14,000 had been amassed. This included a high of 27,000 who had roasted together on the Monday, and a very respectable 10,000 who assembled for the slings and arrows of cricketing fortune on the Wednesday. Throughout the four days these many thousands were clad in what *Wisden* primly termed 'the lightest permissible summer attire'.

A drawn game was for some a just outcome. A more critical view was expressed that England, with three wins to their credit and with the sun beating enervatingly down, were somewhat diffident in attitude, and really should have won convincingly. This opinion balanced the one that suggested that the South Africans should have striven more vigorously in pursuit of the consolation of a victory. The cynic – and, thankfully, he was scarcely to be found in that fulsome summer – might have whispered that the last session of the match characterised the worst of both sides: nondescript bowling to uncertain batting.

England 427 (Hutton 81, Compton 53, Yardley 59, Gladwin 51) and 325 for 6 dec. (Compton 113)
South Africa 302 (Mitchell 120, Dawson 55) and 423 for 7 (Mitchell 189*, Nourse 97)
Match drawn

The Test series, therefore, concluded with three wins for England and two drawn games, and the legend was laid of enormous English supremacy over the visitors. There is no denying some substantial truth in that statement, but, on a match-to-match basis, it might be argued that, had the wheels of fate turned a little differently, the South Africans might have emerged more successfully. They should, on normal considerations, have won the first Test; they were not so overwhelmed in the delightful second Test as the scores maintain, and might well have survived with more self-denial; the third Test could and perhaps should have been drawn; the fourth, oddly, as it was in fashion the least extravagant of the quintet, showed England at their most authoritative; and the fifth might just have been won by the South Africans.

Cricket, like most sports, lacks not for fantasists who can find, among the tinkers' pans of 'ifs' and 'ands', alternative scenarios of what might have been. In 1947 there must have been a few fierce adherents to the South African cause who mused bitterly over the hypothesis that they should have won the series two to one, with two drawn!

The second legend of 1947 was of a shimmering summer, but there were, in fact, phases of wet weather during all the Tests apart from the last, which, perhaps because of its place in the sequence, secured itself in the collective cricketing memory and endowed the rest with a bounty of torpid heat they did not enjoy. It is true the first two Tests were not much disrupted, but the third and fourth certainly turned on the vicissitudes of the climate. The year was not so excessively dry as, for instance, 1921, 1940, 1976, 1989 or 1990, when the absence of any rain at all for long periods was almost eerie. But the magnificent and powerful sunshine of August was unequalled in the memories of all, then and since, and it was this which created the legend.

The third legend involved the contribution of Edrich and Compton, and this cannot be forsworn. There is no denial possible in the face of their combined arithmetic. In all matches against the South Africans the pair scored over 2,000 runs. In the Tests they compiled 1,305 runs: Edrich, 552, average 110; and Compton, 753, average 94. This was not far off a half of the runs – some 3,000 – scored with the bat. Washbrook, Hutton, Evans and Yardley were the only other batsmen of note, each with moderately decent averages, but only Hutton managed a century. There is little doubt what might have happened to the rubber if possibly even one of the Middlesex men had been absent.

Dudley Nourse, Bruce Mitchell and Alan Melville each averaged well over 60 and scored among them seven centuries, the same number that England amassed, that is, four to Compton, two to Edrich and Hutton's one. Mann and Tuckett were their most successful bowlers, with 15 wickets apiece, the one – 350 maidens out of 954 overs – the epitome of accuracy, the other showing immense steadfastness, for he pulled a groin muscle in the first Test, and never quite recovered. Rowan had 12 wickets, but at exorbitant cost. It might well be argued that the tourist attack was superior to that of the home side. Wright was the pick with 19, but Edrich, hurtling into the fray, had 16 wickets, and this was a major feature of the series. Cranston chipped in with 11 victims in the last three matches, and technically climbed to the top of the averages.

The difference is to be seen in the bowlers used, even allowing for the fact that the home side could recruit at will, and the visitors were reduced to choice from their small party. Five bowlers shared the burden for South Africa, and, even under the harshest pressure from Compton and Edrich, they rarely if ever wilted. These were, of course, Tuckett and Dawson to open the attack, to be followed by the spin of Mann, Rowan and Smith. Plimsoll bowled in just one match, and Mitchell bowled two overs at the end of a game. On the other hand, England tried no less than eighteen bowlers, and were not much nearer salvation at the end of that myriad trial. It is surprising that Yardley, who had bowled so well in Australia the previous winter, bowled only six overs, and this might have been a case of undue modesty on the part of the skipper. Aside from Edrich, no rival emerged to capture the role of partnering the resting Bedser with the new ball. Howorth did well in the final Test, and Young was not a failure in the fourth, but neither were fit replacements for Hedley Verity, and right-arm orthodox spin was also lacking. Wright continued to astound with his pacey leg-breaks and googlies – and that reminds us of another curiosity: the South Africans, whose countrymen patented the googly, fielded, for just about the first time since that invention, a side without an exponent of that exotic art.

One wonders how superior England would have been if the South African bowlers had been indigenous, and vice versa. It must also be said that the South African fielding, with Melville and Dawson especially noteworthy, was more alert and safe than that of England, and, whatever the strife, it never caved in, as the English attack and fielding tended to do at Nottingham and the Oval.

A fourth and fifth legend prevailed, and these were also soundly based. One refers to the massive crowds which congregated for these five games. A figure of some 350,000 people watched the series, a staggering audience indeed, and there were plenty of big crowds at many other venues visited by the South Africans. Safety limits and all-seated stadia have restricted crowd numbers over the decades, but it is unlikely that such numbers would assemble, usually in gross discomfort, to watch Tests in England now.

The related legend is of a friendly series. Several players have commented that this rubber was played in a most amiable and sporting fashion, and some have opined that it was the friendliest they had known. There were none of the incidents of disgruntled behaviour that mar today's Test match arenas; there was no defiance of umpires and no ill-tempered gestures of protest. One would like to believe that these two facets – the great crowds and the civilised bonhomie – had an effect upon each other. Certainly the South Africans made a multitude of friends, and they were extremely popular with the crowds which assembled to enjoy their performances.

The South Africans deserved their profits of £10,000, and it was typical of their bearing and character that they should, at Old Trafford and at the Oval, have given a half of their gate receipts toward the repair of those bomb-damaged grounds.

But all was not complete. The Test matches then were compressed into a tighter period, so that, as well as having a longer period of induction and acclimatisation, touring parties had a relaxed phase of post-Test fixtures. They played five more matches; they touched peak batting form; and they won four and drew one.

At a sun-baked Southend, it was nip and tuck after the opening innings, for Cray, Crabtree and Wilcox had helped Essex to a tall score, before South Africa responded with exactly 400. Denis Begbie hit his only century of the tour. On the last day Plimsoll took 7 for 47 in quick time, and the South Africans knocked off the runs with 8 wickets in hand. There was much high scoring at Canterbury, where a Viljoen hundred guided South Africa to over 400. Leading by almost 100 on the first innings, the tourists were able to declare, setting Kent a target of 320, and won by 86 runs. Mann's outstanding match analysis was 13 for 227. The last county match was at Hove. Sussex made a highly presentable 415 for 5, with H. W. Parks and George Cox scoring hundreds. The South Africans, run-getting at a giddy pace, compiled their largest total of the tour: 555 for 6 (Viljoen 201; Melville 114 not out) in an amazing four and a half hours. On a sun-baked pitch and outfield, Sussex batted through most of the last day for a draw.

The South Africans remained, after the Oval Test, in the vicinity of the south-east coast. They next went to Hastings and thrashed the South of England by 9 wickets. The South Africans once more batted brilliantly. This time it was Mitchell and Dawson who scored the hundreds, as they topped 500 for the second time in succession. The South of England made 341 for 9, the historic feature of which was Compton's 101. The South Africans made him struggle, despite the festival nature of the match, but his innings meant that with this, his seventeenth century of the season, he had broken the 1925 record of sixteen hundreds, held by Jack Hobbs. It was his sixth against the tourists, and it seemed apt that Compton should establish his record against those opponents. It still stands (later, in the Champions versus the Rest match he added an eighteenth), and there was much rejoicing among players and crowd. The South Africans would not allow this to baulk them. The follow-on was enforced after Robins's declaration; Mann and Rowan shared the wickets, as the South of England collapsed, leaving South Africa splendid winners.

The fifth and last match was at Guildford, and it was an enjoyable one-day affair played at breakneck speed; 715 runs were scored, with Harris reaching his double-century in a little over two hours. A. C. L. Bennett batted well for the Club Cricket Conference and scored 156, and the match was drawn. As it happened, the South Africans had one fixture remaining, and that was against H. D. G. Levenson Gower's XI at the Scarborough festival. As another stark reminder of those immediate post-war problems, however, shipping conditions were difficult and they had to return home earlier than had been organised. That last game thus had to be cancelled.

Bruce Mitchell was top of their first-class batting averages with 2,014 runs at 61. Viljoen, Nourse and Melville all easily passed the 1,000-run marker, and had averages in the 40s. Dawson was the fifth to 1,000 runs, just scraping in with 1,002. Smith headed the mainline bowling averages, with 58 wickets at 23. Rowan was the only one to take 100 wickets, but his 102 victims cost him 25 runs apiece. Mann (74), Tuckett (69), Plimsoll (58) and Dawson (54) showed admirable consistency, so that all South Africa's six bowlers had reasonable seasons, in spite of the weight of batting laid against them, often in favourable conditions.

5

The County Championship

Like the strong sub-plot of a grand opera or well-crafted novel, the County Championship was evolving in fascinating style alongside the enthralling Test series. In the introductory chapter to this middle section on 1947 proper, the bland neutrality of alphabetical order was carefully chosen to unveil the initial settlement of each county into the 1947 season. After the manner of the announcement of the winners of beauty competitions, we now proceed to discuss each of the seventeen counties in reverse order, using their places in the final Championship table as arbiter. Thus, from the gloomy despair of Northamptonshire to the heady euphoria of Middlesex, one is able to portray the chief elements in a well-fought county contest.

Northamptonshire

A tie with Essex was all Northants had to show for their efforts by the time of the first Test, and their heavy defeat by the South Africans immediately prior to that event proved to be a dark portent. They next lost by a huge margin to Kent at Gravesend, following which rain seemed to be their main ally. Seven of the next eight games were drawn, including a fixture with the Combined Services, but Hampshire, twice, and Surrey could count themselves unlucky to be thwarted by the weather. Warwickshire beat Northants in two days among this cluster of matches, but, at least, as July unfolded, the county's batting firmed up somewhat. Percy Davis regained his form with a fine century against Glamorgan, and then excelled himself with 237 against the weak Somerset side. The old faithful, Dennis Brookes, was another to touch top form at this stage, scoring 169 and 84 not out against Essex and 84 against Somerset. Timms also scored a hundred against Somerset,

Northants reaching a total of 506. They had the better of these two games, and might well have defeated Essex.

Then things went drastically wrong. In fixtures against the stronger counties from the middle of July to the beginning of August, Northants suffered loss after loss. In consecutive games, Lancashire, Gloucestershire, Middlesex (who needed only half an hour on the third day), Derbyshire and Worcestershire trounced them. Brookes had solid hundreds against Lancashire and Middlesex, but, that apart, the batting often disintegrated, and Northants were frequently skittled for low totals. One light shining in a naughty world was the left-arm spin of Vince Broderick, who had played just one match in 1939 before his call to the colours. On a helpful pitch against Derbyshire at Rushden, he returned the amazing analysis of 9.4 overs, 5 maidens, 8 for 16. Even so, Northants contrived to lose by 7 wickets.

It was August, and Northants had no victory and scarcely any points. However, they managed two victories as the weather mended. The first was over Leicestershire at the bank holiday weekend. Brookes was again the mainstay, for, after losing several partners cheaply, Eddie Davis and he produced a county record stand of 259. Brookes scored a double-century and Eddie Davis, younger brother of Percy Davis, enjoyed his maiden century. C. B. Clarke, the West Indian leg-spinner, and R. W. Clarke, a debutant medium-paced bowler, both performed well, as Leicestershire were removed twice. Northants won by 6 wickets.

Their second and, disappointingly, final success of 1947 was at Wellingborough. Here Northants shot out Worcestershire twice in two days and won by 8 wickets. Barron, with 106, made the only substantive contribution on either side, while C. B. Clarke, Broderick and R. J. Partridge, a lively opening bowler, reduced Worcester to totals of 179 and 150. Howorth was the only batsman who seemed able to cope with them, and so, surprisingly, Northants found themselves winners in two games out of three over a ten-day phase.

But these successes seemed to do nothing for the confidence of the Northamptonshire side. They sank dismally to five consecutive losses, as the sun shone and baked the grounds in the last weeks of the season. What is more, they were all fearful drubbings, with

Northants never even sniffing the hint of a draw. Despite the efforts of Brookes, Glamorgan dispatched them twice in two days for an innings victory at Swansea, while a weakened Somerset beat them by 5 wickets at Weston-super-Mare, also in two days. Next, Nottinghamshire won by 336 runs; Yorkshire by 351 runs; and, in a final humiliation at Lord's, Middlesex by 355 runs. Although C. B. Clarke took plenty of wickets in these three games, including 7 for 120 against Yorkshire at Northampton, the batting was embarrassingly woeful. It was pathetically apt that their last innings of the season should be their lowest: 74 against Middlesex. Both this match and the Yorkshire fixture were finished in two days.

Two wins, a tie and as many as seventeen defeats pinned Northants firmly to the foot of the table. Ever-reliable, Brookes, with an average of just under 40, headed the batting by a long way, and only two others scraped past the 1,000-run mark behind him. The captain, A. W. Childs-Clarke, played some valiant knocks, but the only gleam on the horizon was the all-round form of Broderick, with his 768 runs and 75 wickets. C. B. Clarke remained the leading bowler with 83 victims.

Sadly, this was no new situation for them. They had been bottom or second from bottom in twelve of the last thirteen playing seasons. At a time when the Championship had an internal construct of strong and feeble teams, Northants were the weakest, and were often no more than a chopping block for the rest. There was excitement and happiness aplenty in 1947 – but not for Northamptonshire.

Hampshire

The county never really overcame a poor start. June proved to be not too bad a month. Neil McCorkell's century and G. E. M. Heath's bag of 13 wickets paved the way to a stirring win over Derbyshire at Portsmouth, while Sussex were easily disposed of by an innings in Chichester. Heath and V. J. Ransom destroyed Sussex on an awkward pitch in under two days. There were also draws with Yorkshire, Northants and Essex.

Matters deteriorated somewhat in July. After drawing with Cambridge University, Hampshire were beaten by Middlesex in a low-scoring encounter at Portsmouth, being all out for 78 at their second attempt. In a drawn game at Worcester they showed little courage in response to a hospitable declaration. There were draws with Nottinghamshire and with Somerset, both of which were totally ruined by rain. Rogers scored his first Championship hundred in the former, and Hampshire managed first innings lead in the latter.

Essex then visited Bournemouth, and won by the convincing margin of an innings and 108 runs. Heavy guns from the batting department and astute spin bowling was too much for an inept Hampshire team. Perhaps still bemused, Hampshire next found themselves on the end of a 10-wicket thrashing by Glamorgan at Southampton. A third emphatic defeat followed at Canterbury where Kent were the victors by an innings and 44 runs. Having suffered in the field on the Saturday, Hampshire were shot out twice on August bank holiday Monday, although J. E. Manners, playing his first match since 1936, delighted with a century. A lieutenant-commander in the Royal Navy, he was very much in Hampshire's martial tradition of exceptional soldier- or sailor-batsmen who were too rarely available.

Back at Portsmouth, Hampshire enjoyed their last victory of the season, against Surrey. Great batting by Rogers (his 178 was the highest of the season for Hampshire) with McCorkell and Arnold in goodly support enabled them to make a rare declaration. Much heartened, Hampshire made Warwickshire follow on at Southampton, but the Hampshire curse of non-penetrative bowling permitted them to escape. Then there were three more losses away from home, against Somerset, Derbyshire and Lancashire, but the Derbyshire game was close and hard fought. By now Hampshire were well down the table, and their season a grave disappointment. After this short tour they returned to Bournemouth for the last three games of the season, and, in fact, did reasonably well against powerful opponents. There were high-scoring draws with Gloucestershire and Yorkshire, and then Hampshire's first-ever tie, with Lancashire. Consistent batting produced a Hampshire score of 363, to which Lancashire replied with 367 for 9. Hampshire now hurried themselves along to set a challenge of 221 in 135 minutes, and Lancashire picked up the gauntlet. Washbrook and Place made 142 in 90 minutes, but Jim Bailey, who took 6 for 82, engineered a momentous collapse. The Greek dramatic unities converged in their cricketing guise: one over remained; one wicket was left (Lancashire had only ten men); one run was needed. Gerry Hill bowled three balls dead on a length; the fourth was played a little wide of mid-on; and, in the ensuing scuffle, a run out occurred to secure the tie.

Hampshire had not done well in the years before the war, and, although tenth in 1946, their slippage to second but last in the table was not unexpected. They lacked bowlers. Knott and Herman were less successful than in the previous year, and Jim Bailey, whilst taking 51 wickets, was often expensive. Heath grafted industriously and took 74 wickets, whereas Ransom, in his first season with Hampshire, topped the averages with 54 victims. The batting was much more dependable, albeit a little too reliant on McCorkell, Arnold and Rogers. This hardy trio each scored over 1,500 runs and averaged over 35. The next best total was the enthusiastic Desmond Eagar with 980 runs at 26. Under his exemplary lead – he took thirty-four catches – fielding remained Hampshire's most consistent feature. It was to be the late 1950s before the county became genuine contenders for the Championship.

Warwickshire

After being in poor positions in the late 1930s and again in 1946, Warwickshire looked for brighter prospects in 1947, and at first hopes seemed well founded. They had won three and lost five at the start of June, and they should have come near to balancing those scales by beating Gloucestershire at Birmingham. Taylor and Ord scored centuries to place Warwickshire in a superior position, but Gloucester rallied twice, first from a first innings collapse, and then by saving the game with 9 wickets down. Fred Gardner made a sturdy debut to his long career of obdurate batsmanship.

A draw followed with Nottinghamshire, then they were beaten by Cambridge University, having been 19 for 5 and all out for 77 at their first and quite humiliating attempt. At Blackpool they were lucky to draw with Lancashire, while back at Birmingham they won their fourth victory of the season, and their first at home, a frail Northants team being the losers. Pritchard, the New Zealander, was

The South African touring team during a break for rain in the first match of the tour, Worcester, April 30.
Back row (from left): J. Lindsay, A. Rowan, J. Plimsoll, L. Tuckett, N. Mann, D. Begbie.
Front row (from left): K. Viljoen, D. Nourse, A. Melville, B. Mitchell, D. Dyer.

South Africa's off-spinner, Athol Rowan, bowling at Worcester, April 30. The sparse crowd in the background suggests that that April was certainly not a part of any sun-drenched summer.

Norman 'Tufty' Mann bowling for the South Africans against Cambridge University in May, in the relaxed surroundings of Fenners.

Dudley Nourse is bowled by J. W. Martin in the gloom of Lord's on the second day of the tourists' match against MCC. Martin played only seven first-class matches in 1947, one of which was the first Test against South Africa.

Bill Edrich steps down the wicket to drive a ball from Smith during his first-innings 57 in the first Test at Trent Bridge. The only other contribution of note came from Edrich's sparring partner, Denis Compton, and England were forced to follow on.

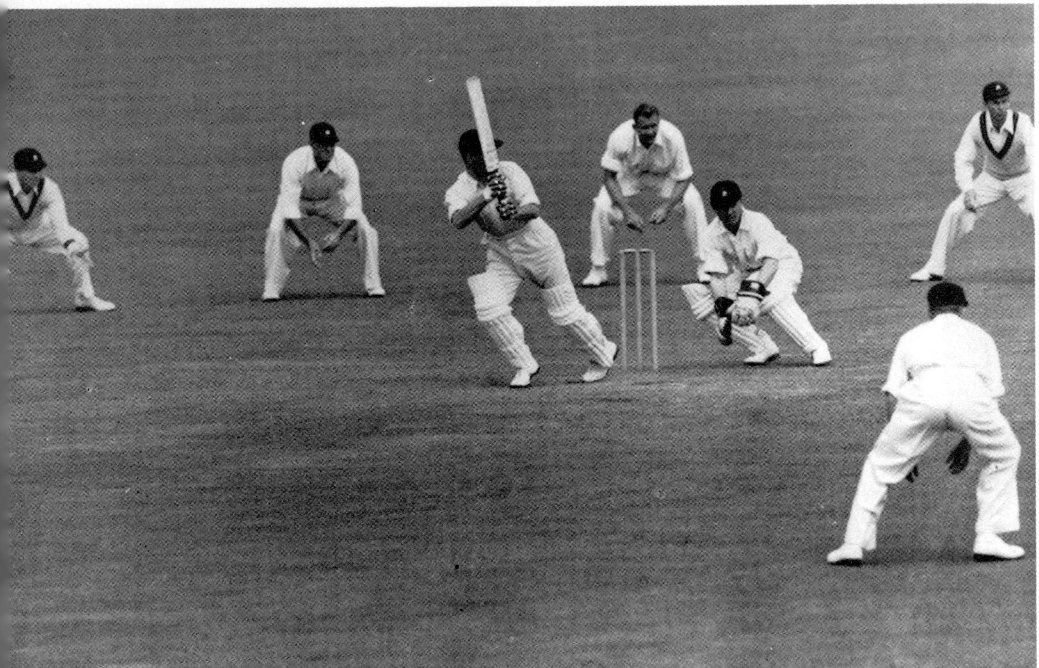

Skittled out for 208 in the first Test at Trent Bridge, England's batsmen fought back in the second innings to reach 551. Here Norman Yardley, dropped by Mitchell early in his innings, plays to leg through a crowded close field in the course of an invaluable 99.

In reply to England's huge total of 554 in the second Test at Lord's, South Africa's resistance was led by Alan Melville, with 117, and Dudley Nourse. Here Nourse pulls Derbyshire's George Pope over the leg trap during the first of his two half-centuries in the match.

South Africa's captain, Alan Melville, and debutant Dennis Dyer walk out to open the innings in the fourth Test at Headingley. Dyer, who otherwise endured a miserable tour, made 62.

Alan Melville drives Middlesex spinner Jack Young through the covers on the third day of the fourth Test. Although Melville and Nourse fought to provide substance to South Africa's second innings, they could not prevent an England win by 7 wickets.

Spectator interest in all cricket, but especially in the Test matches, was phenomenal throughout 1947. As the hot weather reached a peak in August, so the queues extended all the way round the Oval and beyond for the final Test against South Africa.

As England sought to declare in the second innings of the final Test, Denis Compton scored 113 in less than two hours, out of 178 scored while he was at the wicket.

Bruce Mitchell pushes the single that brought up his second-innings century in the final Test, to emulate the feat of his captain, Melville, in scoring two hundreds in one Test.

In a summer when runs flowed like wine, the 47-year-old Tom Goddard of Gloucestershire bucked the trend by taking the extraordinary number of 238 first-class wickets at 17 runs apiece. Here he turns his off-breaks in a county match against Surrey at a relaxed Oval.

The redoubtable John Ikin of Lancashire showed fine all-round form to finish the 1947 season with over 1,000 runs and 48 first-class wickets, including a match haul of 11–119 against Nottinghamshire. His absence from the Test scene left England short of a high-quality fieldsman.

Doug Wright took 177 first-class wickets during the summer at a cost (21.12) incredibly low for a leg-spinner. Omitted from the first Test, he confounded the selectors with 11 wickets for Kent against Northamptonshire, to win back his international place for the rest of the series.

Winston Place forged a formidable opening partnership with Cyril Washbrook for Lancashire, both scoring over 2,500 runs at averages over 60. While Washbrook held his Test place against South Africa, Place's reward came in the winter with a tour to the West Indies and a Test century there.

Bill Edrich puts on his blazer while waiting to bat. His brilliant batting feats were underpinned by an ability with the ball which brought him 47 wickets for Middlesex and the new ball in an England attack bereft of genuine pace.

The England selectors' neglect of Nottinghamshire's Joe Hardstaff seems particularly short-sighted when his 2,396 runs at an average of nearly 70 are considered against the failure of his Test replacements, Dollery and Barnett. Although approaching the veteran stage, his end-of-season form reflected continuing stamina and determination.

Although Lancashire's Ken Cranston enjoyed a statistically modest season in 1947, his all-round ability in his short career at the top won him a Test place against South Africa and the vice-captaincy on the winter tour to West Indies. Here he drives the teenage leg-spinner, Ian Bedford, during a match against Middlesex. Leslie Compton is the wicket-keeper.

The Middlesex team of all the talents that won the County Championship in 1947.
Back row (from left): I. Bedford, R. Thompson, L. H. Gray, L. H. Compton, J. D. B. Robertson, S. M. Brown, J. A. Young.
Front row (from left): W. J. Edrich, F. G. Mann, R. W. V. Robins, J. M. Sims, D. C. S. Compton.

enjoying his first full English season, and he took 8 wickets in a low-scoring game, Eric Hollies capturing 11.

There was a draw at Swansea, and at Coventry Essex ended comparatively unstressed winners on a lively track. It was Ord – with rain a welcome ally – who saved the next game for Warwickshire, for his patient 35, over two hours, stemmed Lancashire's advance when, as at Blackpool, they had been well placed.

Two valuable and heartening victories were in the offing. First, Sussex were defeated by 174 runs and then rain and low scores created an exciting match with Kent at Birmingham. Kent required 111 but, after the expected mix of thrills and spills, Warwickshire won by 8 runs. Hollies had match figures of 10 for 96.

It was the middle of July and, with six wins amid flurries of draws in those rain-affected weeks, Warwickshire were perhaps startled to find themselves sixth in the table. It was a false position, as was soon demonstrated. Warwicks never won another game in the County Championship. Their only consolation was a victory, adjudged first-class, against the Scottish Cricket Union. They had two draws hereabouts with Derbyshire and Hampshire. In both instances Warwickshire had to follow on, and in both instances it was the valiance of Ord, with 111 and 88, who rescued them.

It was apparent that Warwickshire were powerless and out of sorts. The two remaining home games ended in defeat. Surrey disposed of them summarily by 6 wickets with time to spare, and Sussex beat them by 151 runs. It must have been in sad heart that Warwickshire took to the road for their last three matches, and in fact they lost all of them, ending the season with five successive defeats and finishing fifteenth in the table. The Yorkshire match proved to be close-run, but they lost to Leicestershire by the wide gap of 120 runs. In a final exhibition of diffident bowling, Warwickshire contrived to capture only 8 Nottinghamshire wickets in both innings at Trent Bridge.

Thus ended a summer sunk in disappointment. Ord, Taylor, Dollery and W. A. Hill each passed a 1,000 runs but none of them scored excessively and only Ord touched 30 in average. Dollery, who kept wicket capably for the larger section of the season, fell away in his batting, and much the same happened to Hollies and his bowling. Although he took 95 wickets, including several sizeable hauls, it was a far cry from his 175 in 1946. Pritchard bowled as fast as anybody on the county circuit and took 87 wickets, suffering a few strains as he underwent the rigours of a lengthy season. Grove, with a pleasing 86 wickets, and Cannings, with 61 wickets, were the two other bowlers of note, but plainly Warwickshire in 1947 were at sixes and sevens. They had several journeymen, but not one of them plied his trade above the level of ordinariness. No one scored 1,500 runs or took 100 wickets.

Happily one may now see that this was the last of the bad times for Warwickshire for some years, and that those competent tradesmen were soon to gel into a coherently tough side. The 1951 Championship would be their monument.

Leicestershire

Often one of the whipping-boys of the county competition, Leicestershire had been eleventh in 1946, a reasonable spot for a county of their resources and aspirations. In 1947, however, they fell to fourteenth. It was the more disappointing in that they had a bright start. They had won three games almost before June had arrived – but they were to win only three more throughout the season. What is more, they lost fourteen times, and won only one match in the whole of June and July.

Despite a century from V. E. Jackson, Gloucestershire found them easy meat at the time of the first Test, while at Loughborough Kent beat them by 52 runs in a game reduced by rain to two days. Walsh and Jackson bowled assiduously enough, but the batting went all awry. Derbyshire next beat them at Ilkeston by the shaming margin of an innings and 105 runs, Maurice Tompkin's 61 being the only score above 33 in either innings. At Bath Somerset were the victors by 100 runs, but then came the solitary victory of this all but barren phase. G. S. Watson apart, the Leicester batting failed twice, and left Worcestershire needing only 123 runs to win. Jack Walsh bamboozled his opponents to such an extent with his leg-breaks and googlies that he took 6 for 18; they were all out for 80.

Two games with Lancashire came next, and both ended in defeats, by 5 and by 10 wickets. A welcome draw was managed with Glamorgan at Swansea. There was no play on the first day, and the game was basically a personal tournament between slow bowlers, Walsh taking 7 for 53 and earning his county some much needed first innings points. A curio was that Jack Lee, the Leicester City and England footballer, took a wicket with the first ball of his only spell of bowling in his one and only first-class game.

The Middlesex visit to Leicester was one to savour, and their 10-wicket victory was one of their most enthralling of the season. However, Leicestershire did proffer some of their better batting of the season, with Les Berry scoring 53 and 154, Jackson 117, Riddington 63 and Tompkin 76. Two more draws followed against Yorkshire and Warwickshire; Gloucestershire then won by 71 runs; but as July turned toward August, Leicestershire recorded their most thrilling win of the season, against Derbyshire at Leicester. Derbyshire set them 391 runs for victory, and they were 236 for 6 with less than two hours remaining. Then Vic Jackson and H. G. Pickering hit the strong attack with virile abandon; 7 were needed as the last over began; Jackson straight drove Gladwin's third delivery for a resounding 6; and Leicester had won against the odds by 3 wickets.

It was down to earth for the bank holiday clash with lowly Northants, who won by 6 wickets, their first success at Leicester for twenty years. It was much the same story, if less unexpected, in the following game, with Yorkshire. Once more Leicestershire were made to follow on, and they lost by an innings and 4 runs.

At Clacton they drew with Essex in a match which was distinguished by Berry's fine performance of a century in each innings, 165 and 111 not out. At Hastings, poor Sussex bowling enabled Leicestershire to amass a huge score: 547, still their largest total since the war. At Dover, Kent pulverised them, only Jackson's first innings century redeeming a ragged display.

Returning to Leicester, the county let the Somerset game slip away from them after an excellent beginning, Tompkin and Lester scoring hundreds in a total of 454. Amends were at hand with a stout victory by 120 runs over Warwickshire, a victory which enabled Leicestershire to push ahead of Warwickshire in the final table. In the last game of the season Surrey trounced them by an innings and 201 runs.

For the first time in their history, six batsmen reached 1,000 runs in all first-class fixtures: Berry, Tompkin, Jackson, Prentice, Watson and Lester. Les Berry scored 1,733, and aside from his four centuries he scored with sound consistency. Although, rightly, Dollery is thought of as the first of the modern, omnicompetent professional captains, Berry was the Leicester skipper for the seasons 1946–48, and he could take pride in having helped break the traditional amateur domination. In demeanour and role, he was the twin of Brookes, the Northants opener, in that both commanded great respect while playing for inferior teams, where they often stood bloodied but unbowed as lesser mortals collapsed around them.

Similarly, while the Leicester bowling was frequently savaged (and the fielding, the wicket-keeping of Paddy Corrall excepted, placed under intolerable stress) there were stand-out displays. Walsh took 142 wickets at an average of just under 23, and, when it came to 'reading' bowlers, he was widely regarded as perhaps the most illegible on the circuit. He was selected for the Players against the Gentlemen. But it was significant that the Leicester opening attack was often composed of the useful medium pace of Sperry, who took 71 wickets, and the off-breaks of Jackson, who took 76. There was no speed to speak of, and, beyond those three, precious few bowling reserves. It was indeed the stalwart all-round skills of Jackson – like Walsh a native of Sydney – which helped prise Leicestershire from the very bottom.

Leicestershire were, fundamentally, three or four players short of a respectable side. They were to have pleasant seasons (notably when they soared to third place in 1953) but, by and large, they were to hug the bottom rungs of the ladder for many years to come.

Somerset

By each compiling exactly 100 points, Essex, Nottinghamshire and Somerset shared eleventh place in the county table, separated there only by alphabetic determination. Having been fourth in 1946 – their best placement since the enlargement of the Championship – Somerset enjoyed high expectations of 1947. These were dashed. Somerset won eight, but lost twelve, and they managed first innings points from only one of their lost and drawn games. Like

Leicestershire, they were to spend most of the next several seasons at or near the bottom of the county table.

After a 1-wicket win against Middlesex at the start of the season, not another win was negotiated until the last week of June. As the month dawned, there was an innings defeat at Leeds, with only Gimblett's batting and the captain R. J. O. Meyer's bowling holding up Yorkshire. A visit to Chesterfield brought humiliation, the first county match completed in a day since 1925. Timid and bewildered beyond belief, Somerset were out for 68 and 38, and Derbyshire flattened them by an innings and 125 runs.

After nine consecutive defeats, the county must have been extremely pleased to find Leicestershire in dispirited form. The batting of Gimblett and Buse and the bowling of Wellard and Tremlett enabled them to prevail by 100 runs. Following a rain-sodden draw with Cambridge University, in which Buse bowled splendidly for his 6 for 37, Somerset struck again. This time their opponents were Worcestershire, and in a low-scoring encounter Wellard, mixing quick swing and slow off-spin, took 15 for 101, one of the most noteworthy displays of the summer. Somerset won by 4 wickets.

Draws followed with Worcester, Nottingham and Northants, the last featuring 88 and 113 not out from the brilliant and evergreen Gimblett. They completed the double over Middlesex, weakened by the calls of the Players and Gentlemen fixture, drew with Hampshire at Bournemouth, where that select resort was so wet that only first innings points could be claimed, and then lost to Kent by 7 wickets. The amateur, N. S. Mitchell-Innes, was now available, and his half century was the only solace Somerset had as they were outplayed and outgunned. But there was a surprise in store: Somerset inflicted on Lancashire their only defeat of the summer. The injured Gimblett gamely scored 64, and Horace Hazell took 6 for 51; the leading performances in that hard-won 34-run victory.

It was now into August. First, Gloucestershire inflicted a mammoth defeat upon them, by 316 runs; Somerset were out for 98 and 25, the latter being the lowest score of the season. Next, they drew with Nottingham in a game of mighty scores, to which Gimblett contributed a century and M. M. Walford, the former Oxford Blue lately joining the side, 96. He further distinguished himself in the third August fixture, for his 90 and 101 helped set up an exciting finish, with Glamorgan narrowly the victors. This was the first of the three Weston-super-Mare festival games. Somerset won the second, against Hampshire, by 9 wickets, and here Walford excelled himself with a matchless 264, one of the summer's most memorable demonstrations of powerful driving. Somerset topped 500 in their first innings. The third match was also won, and again Walford was the star. His undefeated 72 ensured a 5-wicket victory, after incisive bowling, first from Meyer and then from Hazell.

Much encouraged, Somerset journeyed to Leicester. Yet another amateur, G. E. S. Woodhouse, who had been an outstanding schoolboy cricketer at Marlborough, and was soon to captain the county, scored a century and thus averted the follow-on. But it was his amateur colleagues, Mitchell-Innes and Walford, whose splendid batting reaped the reward of a 6-wicket win. There followed F. S. Lee's benefit match at Taunton. The beneficiary had had a miserable year, managing only a little more than 500 runs and losing his place. He was rewarded for his pains and fortitude over many years with Somerset's best benefit to date. Hazell bowled well, but the side never came properly to grips with a strong Kent combine, and Somerset were lucky to escape with a draw. Such luck was at a premium for the final match of the year, for Surrey dealt most severely with them, crushing them by an innings.

So ended a curious summer for Somerset. Their old difficulty of fielding settled teams was highlighted by Walford's bravura display, in which he scored 942 in only sixteen innings at an average of 67. A Sherborne schoolmaster, he was never to be readily available, and it is salutary to note that no less than fifteen amateurs turned out for Somerset during the season. The fact that Harold Gimblett batted way below his form of 1946, and yet was the only one to score 1,000 runs, sufficiently exposes the frailty of Somerset's batting. The bowling, somewhat creaking with age here and there, was more consistent, with five getting over 40 wickets, the pick of them Arthur Wellard, now in his mid-40s, with 91. After that meteoric start to his career, Maurice Tremlett settled into the routine of the mundane county circuit, and his 63 wickets and almost 600 runs earned him a trip to the West Indies over the coming winter.

Nottinghamshire

It was mediocre bowling which betrayed the Nottinghamshire interest in 1947 and, at one time, threatened complete débâcle. After seven games, Nottingham had only four points, but they dragged themselves to six wins, against six losses, and a rather happier place in the table. Were timorous bowlers not enough of a drawback, Nottinghamshire had to contend with the excessive benignity of their pitch. A cricketing Shaw might well have dubbed Trent Bridge 'Heartbreak House' – only three of fourteen fixtures there were actually finished. An esteemed county between the wars, priding itself on its flowing batting and ferocious bowling, Nottingham were now numbered among the also-rans.

It is thus a dreary tale to gather up as they travelled down to Gravesend, where centuries from W. W. Keeton and C. B. Harris made sure of a draw with Kent; on to Lord's, where they had inadequate resource to counter the Middlesex juggernaut, losing by 7 wickets; and up to Birmingham for a drawn match with Warwickshire, Keeton and Hardstaff hitting centuries in a fixture marred by heavy rain. It was at home at Trent Bridge, and in mid-June, that Notts recorded their first win, and this was at the expense of Kent, by an innings and 17 runs.

At Sheffield, Yorkshire found Notts in a fresh mood of assurance, and, for the first time since 1923, Notts won. A Harris 100 and 10 wickets from Harold Butler, doubtless relieved to find himself in more friendly conditions, created a 185 runs victory. A thunderstorm came to the aid of Gloucestershire as the revitalised Nottingham XI forced them to follow-on. Reg Simpson played wonderfully well for his 153. Victory over Sussex at Hove by 7 wickets was followed by a straight fight for first innings points against Lancashire; Nottingham prevailed, with centuries from Keeton and Simpson. There were three further draws. The first was with Somerset at Wells, where rain interfered constantly; the second was an overcautious affair with Yorkshire, in which Harris scored another hundred; and the third – with Hampshire – was entirely damaged by the weather.

That meant nine games without defeat. It could not last. Now there were two consecutive defeats, the first, by a mere 15 runs, at the hands of Derbyshire, in which game Butler took 11 for 115; and the second an anticipated Middlesex hammering by 287 runs. Even the normally reliable batting was worn down by the skills of the eventual champions. However, August bank holiday weekend at the Oval brought cheerier pickings, for Surrey were beaten by 48 runs.

Chief compilers of a huge total of 585 in a drawn match with Somerset were Keeton, 113; Simpson, 90; and Hardstaff, not out 200. And then Winrow, 204, and Harvey, 125, joined in an undefeated stand when Derbyshire looked likely winners. Another double century from the prolific Hardstaff, who scored 1,000 runs in August, was the main excitement in a drawn match with Worcestershire, and then Lancashire beat them comfortably at Manchester by 84 runs. The season ended much more pleasingly than it had begun. Northants were overwhelmed by 236 runs. The Nottingham quick bowlers did their manful duty, while Willatt and, yet again, Hardstaff scored good hundreds. Notts had slightly the better of the draw with Glamorgan; Hardstaff and Simpson made their usual hundreds, but the bowlers could not drive home the advantage. Nonetheless, there was a win in the last match, when Warwickshire were beaten by 8 wickets. An early collapse was checked by Hardstaff's third double century of the month – he was undefeated, and was also 45 not out in the second innings. Butler and Jepson, like Hardstaff, completed their seasons typically, sharing 14 wickets.

Even a cursory summary such as this underlines the strength of the Nottingham batsmanship and the corresponding weakness of the bowling. Jepson took 110 wickets, and Butler 87, something of a minor miracle in itself, and a matter of enormous credit to that perspiring and indomitable pair. Winrow, bowling rather expensive left-hand spinners, captured a further 56, while the remainder – and twelve were tried – could muster but 72 wickets all told. Obviously, the abrupt retirement of Bill Voce, Harold Larwood's old partner, was an early blow. He played only five games.

Conversely, the batting, and not only on the featherbed of Trent Bridge, was prodigious, and almost always someone came off. Frequently it was Hardstaff. That most handsome of strikers had a remarkable season and, but for the dramatics of Edrich and

Compton, 1947 might have been labelled Hardstaff's summer. His 2,396 runs (2,230 for the county) left him high in the national averages, and well on top of the county list. But it was five centuries, three of them doubles, in his last eleven innings, when some players of Hardstaff's age might have been forgiven signs of fatigue, that gave his season an epic quality. Four others – Winrow, a useful all-rounder, Keeton, Simpson and Reddick –scored 1,000 runs, and Keeton notched six hundreds. Eight players scored at least one century during the season. It is worth recalling that Somerset, the equal of Notts in Championship points, had only one batsman with 1,000 runs. Harris had 800 runs and three centuries in fifteen matches, and altogether ten players with a minimum of 17 innings averaged over 20.

Nottinghamshire, with the exception of one or two seasons, were to do no better, and often much worse, for many years. And the abiding question must remain: why was Joe Hardstaff not chosen for England, especially as such men as Dollery and Barnett were largely unsuccessful?

Essex

Although it was to be the late 1970s before Essex reached regular prominence in English cricket, it is perhaps forgotten that they had enjoyed a mild success in the 1930s. For a county of unfashionable background and low reserves, they had soldiered on hardily to remain in the top half of the table for most of those years. It was, therefore, after being eighth in 1946, something of a shock to find them hovering, with Somerset and Notts, in the eleventh, twelfth and thirteenth positions, their worst performance since 1932. However, apart from some medium-rated seasons around the turn of the 1950s, this was to be their customary lot. It was the more distressing in that Essex had now recruited a membership of over 3,000, their biggest ever, and fine crowds turned up for many of their fixtures.

In early June Essex were defeated by Sussex. Morris and Dines enjoyed a commendable ninth wicket stand of 111, but Sussex won with 5 wickets if only ten minutes to spare. There was a draw with Lancashire: rain and the obstinacy of the Essex captain, Tom

Pearce, were the saviours. At Cardiff, Glamorgan won by an innings, Ray Smith's bag of 5 wickets the only twinkling memory from a dark three days.

The good news was just around the corner. Middlesex, their powers diluted by Test calls, succumbed by 10 wickets. The villain of the piece, from the Middlesex standpoint, was Peter Smith. His leg-breaks led to an analysis of 16 for 215, by any standards a sterling display. He next took 7 for 129 against Hampshire, but only thunderstorms over Colchester saved Essex after an inept performance. It was a see-saw season for Essex. Recovering themselves, they beat Warwickshire by 6 wickets, and after a draw with Northampton – a well-balanced encounter in doubt until the last half-hour – Gloucestershire were meritorious winners at Westcliff. Vigar took 5 for 68, and the batting was not disgraced, but Gloucester were simply the more accomplished. The second match of the Westcliff week was drawn, the weather once more intervening. Glamorgan took first innings points, but Avery batted courageously, in spite of an injured knee; and Peter Smith, with 5 wickets in each innings (reducing the Welsh visitors to 95 for 5 when they altered their batting order in the closing hours) reached 100 wickets. It was only 18 July – and this was supposed to be a batsman's summer.

Middlesex took their predictable vengeance, winning by a margin of 102 runs. Essex were combative enough. Consistent batting (a feature of their season) brought seemly totals of 350 and 293. Essex, rightfully undismayed, journeyed to Bournemouth, and treated Hampshire with scant ceremony. Horsfall, 170, and Vigar, 125, put on 225 for the third wicket, and everyone else contributed generously to a total of 532. There were 9 wickets for the wily Peter Smith, and an overwhelming victory – by an innings and 108 runs. There were runs perhaps in overabundance at Maidstone, where only sixteen wickets fell, and where S. J. Cray's century was one of several big scores. That draw was the prelude to another defeat, a close one, by 2 wickets, by Surrey, in a game that Essex should have won easily. Tempestuous storms disrupted the holiday game with Worcestershire at Chelmsford, but the visitors were not distracted. They required only 17 runs in their second innings, Essex having ignominiously been shot out for 65 in their first innings. The switchback of fortunes continued. There was a fine win by 5 wickets at Chesterfield. Trevor Bailey, having recently joined the side from Cambridge University, took 5 wickets in each innings, but the drama lay in the record tenth-wicket stand for Essex. Vigar, with 114 not out in five hours, was manifestly outpaced by the feisty Peter Smith, who smashed an amazing 163 in short order, including 22 in one over. They added 218, and rarely can a No. 11 batsman have been so domineering, and certainly none has scored so many runs.

There was an enthralling battle for first innings points at Clacton, where, with 400 for 9, Essex just edged past Leicestershire, but the second match of the Clacton festival saw Lancashire emerge as comfortable winners. Ray Smith took 6 for 152, and that extravagant analysis summed up the situation. Essex lost by an innings. They drew with Sussex around the coast at Eastbourne and their star was Trevor Bailey, who scored 205. His later admirers will not be surprised to learn that his first hundred runs were grafted out over three hours: it may startle some to find that his second hundred was struck in 80 minutes.

Essex ended their summer at Southend. They welcomed Yorkshire for Peter Smith's benefit match, watched by some 7,000 paying spectators who might have been more numerous had not Yorkshire's colours been so bedraggled. However, Peter Smith delighted all by scoring his 1,000th run and thereby completing the double. In a rather unsatisfactory draw, he crowned a glorious season with 6 for 119.

The county, with six wins and ten losses, probably deserved better. The batting only failed drastically on a couple of occasions, and was normally sound. Bailey topped the averages, having done more with bat than ball in his ten games. Pearce, T. C. Dodds, in his first year as a professional, F. H. Vigar and Ray Smith reached the 1,000-run mark for the county, and six batsmen averaged over 30. There were some disappointments. Douglas Insole, another Cambridge Blue soon to play for England, did little, and the Yorkshire immigrant, Horsfall, fell away a trifle. Although Vigar gave sturdy support with 59 wickets, the bowling was almost entirely monopolised by the Smiths. Both completed the double. Ray, in all first-class matches, had 1,386 runs and 125 wickets; Peter had 1,065 runs and 172 wickets, the highest number ever for an

Essex bowler. It must freely be confessed that with averages of 37 and 27 respectively, they were far from being the most economical of bowlers; yet the mix of quick stuff and off-spin of the one, and the inventive array of wrist spin of the other, formed the bulk of the Essex attack. These were not the least interesting aspects of a multivaried season.

Sussex

Sussex shared ninth spot with Glamorgan and, captained for the first time by the attacking left-hander, Hugh Bartlett, they showed much improvement on 1946, when they had been bottom. This had been by far their worst performance during a long and illustrious history, and a dismal comedown from their deeds of the early 1930s, when they were thrice runners-up. A tall, good-looking and popular captain, Bartlett ensured that the fielding was up to scratch and that the batting was enterprising – but he could do little or nothing about the bowling. Fifteen times 300 runs or more were hit against them. Like most counties they lacked the penetration of testing pace. It was six batsmen with 1,000 runs apiece who gave Sussex some breathing space.

They won nine and lost twelve in the Championship. One of the victories was in early June at Brentwood, in a match which illustrates the point. H. W. Parks had a century and, with solid all-round batting, Essex were disposed of by 5 wickets, in spite of scoring well themselves. Conversely, uneven batting – Parks, with another glorious century, excepted – at Horsham allowed Worcestershire to gain a 6-wicket win, for there was no compensating high-grade bowling. There was defeat too in the second Horsham engagement. Derbyshire won with some comfort, as, once more, the Sussex batting failed to shine any more brightly than did the sun in a rainy week.

Another rain-spoilt match brought a draw with Surrey, Bartlett's engaging 92 and a brisk 6 for 80 from Carey providing the sole matters for note. The two Chichester fixtures both ended in mournful defeats, by an innings to Hampshire, and by 152 runs to Oxford University. Basically, the Sussex batting failed badly on four consecutive occasions. There was something of a revival at Tunbridge Wells where Kent were beaten by 6 wickets, and where

Jack Cornford took 6 for 74 and John Langridge scored a valuable 138 not out. The Gloucestershire match at Bristol, marred by rainfall, was a draw despite Charlie Oakes scoring 117 not out on the last day, albeit against second-string bowling. The leg-spinner, G. T. Hurst, took 6 for 80 against Warwickshire, but they ran out winners as the Sussex batting again failed.

Sussex collapsed once more against Glamorgan, but then were wonderfully redeemed by a second-innings chase for 376 and an improbable 5-wicket win. Behind by 145 on the first innings and 40 for 3 in the second: that was the stage upon which George Cox strode, for it was his stupendous 205 not out in just over four hours that so theatrically turned the tables. However, one should not, amid the memory of that colourful innings, forget how Carey finished off Glamorgan's first endeavours with a hat-trick.

This mix of the good, the bad and the indifferent continued. A draw with Worcestershire was followed by defeats by Glamorgan and Middlesex. The latter was James Langridge's benefit match. On returning from Australia, and in spite of injury, he had struck decent form only to be afflicted by appendicitis during the first week of June. He had returned to the side barely in time for his benefit, but his unlucky season was rewarded with a sum of over £4,000, by far the richest for a Sussex player at that time.

Northants were then beaten comfortably, but at the run-glutted Hastings festival Sussex first lost to Kent and then, after Parks and both the Langridge brothers scored centuries on a hard-baked pitch, drew with Leicestershire. Next there was a win over Warwickshire by 151 runs; most of the players made a steadfast contribution, none more so than Jack Oakes, whose 7 for 64 was the best of his career.

At Eastbourne, although following on against Essex, they had no trouble saving the game for Cox scored 186, and most of the other batsmen did well in favourable conditions. Charlie Oakes had tried to bolster the first innings with a patient century. Lancashire then defeated them despite hundreds from H. W. Parks and George Cox, but Sussex finished the season with a flourish, beating the fancied Gloucestershire by 9 wickets at Hove. Cox scored his third hundred in as many games; John Langridge was the soul of batting propriety in both innings; and J. K. Nye took 6 for 95.

Feasts of runs in August had augmented the batting averages deliciously. John Langridge headed them with 1,888 runs and an average of 41, a most steady and professional performance which included only three centuries but scarcely a failure. Overcoming his illness bravely, brother James reached his 1,000 runs in only sixteen games, but it was his bowling – only 19 victims – or lack of it that made a major difference. Parks, Cox with six centuries, Charlie Oakes and Bartlett averaged over 30 and passed the 1000-run mark with plenty to spare. A curtain might better be drawn over the corresponding bowling figures. Eighteen players turned their arm, but only Cornford, who had fared poorly in 1946 and who now captured 94 wickets, had no reason to blush.

All in all it was a summer in which Sussex frequently, though not always, unleashed some heavy artillery, but in which they had little protection against the big guns of others.

Glamorgan

Glamorgan were the most junior and one of the least successful counties, with to date only three single-figure placements in the Championship. Indeed, by being sixth in the first season after the war, they had risen to their highest point yet, and so ninth place in 1947 was no mean achievement. They equitably won and lost eight games.

There was a new leader in Wilfred Wooller, Welsh rugby international and survivor of torrid times in Japanese hands. The vigour of his bowling, batting and fielding was no more than a direct representation of his energetic and mettlesome personality, and he must take credit for the part-success of Glamorgan in this summer.

Even without their stars, lost to the first Test, Middlesex proved too tough for Glamorgan at Lord's, although Wooller's cache of 11 wickets gave them something to ponder. Up at Liverpool, it was the last-wicket stand of Porter and Clay in the first innings, and the unbroken partnership of Wooller, with 108, and W. E. Jones, with 90, that saved that match. Another draw followed, against Gloucestershire. There was no play on the Saturday, but Monday's cricket resembled a skittle alley, wickets tumbling indiscriminately. L. B. Muncer, formerly of Middlesex and the coming hero of 1948, took 5 for 51, but, with scores of only 90 and 129 for 7, Glamorgan had A. H. Dyson's grim rearguard action to thank for fortunate survival.

It was, therefore, quite advanced into June before Glamorgan won for the first time since early season, but they did so with substantial emphasis, beating Essex by an innings. Emrys Davies and W. E. Jones, with centuries, led Glamorgan to their highest score of the season – 442 – while the latter's 4 wickets helped dismiss Essex cheaply in their second innings. However, at the Oval Surrey won by an innings, helped by some less than typical untidy fielding. Next, it was Glamorgan's turn again. They beat the strong Kent outfit by an innings and 53 runs. A Dyson century and a solid total of 427 was more than enough for Kent, troubled first by the old-headed cunning of Clay, 6 for 70, and second by the sprightly off-breaks of Wat Jones, 7 for 92.

Glamorgan almost navigated their way through July without a win. They lost to Derbyshire after Wooller, who had a splendid game with bat and ball, set a challenging target, and they drew with Warwickshire in a game drastically curtailed by rain. A Dyson hundred was the only act of any moment. There were draws with Northants and with Leicester, teams one might have expected Glamorgan to beat. The Ebbw Vale ground was packed with 8,000 spectators for Worcestershire's visit, and another draw resulted. Watkins obliged with a century, and Glamorgan managed to capture 7 wickets as their opponents picked up the gauntlet of an opportune declaration. It was a bright, not a dull, draw. Through no fault of the players, the next two draws were depressing. After buoyant batting against Essex, the match was marooned by the weather, whilst the Lancashire match at Cardiff hardly struggled into the second day. In between these two moist encounters, Glamorgan lost to Sussex, and disappointingly so in that Dyson and Davies, with a century each, had opened with a stand of 236 in even time, Wooller had taken 5 for 58, and a first innings lead of 145 had been established.

It was now the last week of July, and Glamorgan contrived to fit in two good wins. They must have enjoyed asking Sussex to follow on, some recompense for the upheavals at Hove the previous week. Dyson, with another century, and Emrys Davies shared in two three-figure stands, but Sussex did manage to hang on until four minutes from time in a fascinating finish. At Southampton, Hampshire were more lamblike in submission, Glamorgan winning by 10 wickets. This time Davies scored a century, but Dyson was only 4 short, as the Glamorgan openers put on 201. Wooller had match figures of 9 for 96.

The county next lost a close game with Worcestershire by a mere 14 runs. In truth, Muncer's spellbinding 5 for 17 and Davies's resilient 177 had given Glamorgan what appeared to be a complete rein on the game, but, rather like the first Sussex match, things then went awry. Still, two victories made up for this loss of control. A most consistent batting display was the platform for a two-day win over Northamptonshire, with Muncer and Clay sharing 14 wickets, and Alan Watkins pouching some remarkable catches close to the wicket. In the last home game, at Cardiff, Muncer was even more definitively to the fore. After a Watkins century had placed Glamorgan in a strong position, he took 9 for 97, the best performance of his career, and Surrey lost by 4 wickets.

The last two matches were at Cheltenham and Nottingham. Gloucestershire won the first by 29 runs. It was a low-scoring affair, in which Muncer, his flight and precision during these days quite unnerving, took 8 for 36. The second was a high-scoring draw, which caused Glamorgan but little anxiety. Dyson and Davies opened with 96, and, in the second innings, Emrys Davies scored a century. Clift, in the last two hours of a dying game and season, hit his first hundred in first-class cricket.

Glamorgan, the equal of Sussex on points, were a much more balanced team, as the events of 1948 were to demonstrate. Davies, who became the first Glamorgan player to score five hundreds in a season, led the averages, just ahead of his sparring partner, Arnold Dyson. These two, the dignified Welshman and the precise Yorkshireman, had shown themselves to be one of the best opening partnerships in the country. Alan Watkins, that epitome of close-order fielding and catching, who was to play for England against the Australians the following year, also scored 1,000 runs. If the batting was not as formidable as that of Sussex, the all-round play was most commendable. Muncer (101 wickets and 868 runs) and Wooller (1,039 runs and 75 wickets) were near to doubles. Clay took 54 wickets, average just under 16, in no more than eleven matches, and

Emrys Davies, with his left-hand spin, gained 47 wickets. The burly Haydn Davies kept wicket efficiently, despite missing some games with an injured hand.

There were a couple of faults, for Wales was not free of the English disease. Umpteen bowlers were tried as partners for Wooller at the start of the attack: Glamorgan had no one of any pace. Non-coincidentally, they were also an ageing side. Wooller himself was nearly 35, the resolute openers were in their early 40s, and J. C. Clay was in his 50th year. Even Watkins, whom one tends to think of as a tyro, at that stage, was 27. Nonetheless, it had not been too bad a year for the Welshmen. Especially is this so if one recalls their misfortunes with the weather: ironically, in a summer hailed for its aridity and warmth, the valleys suffered incessant rain, right through to the end of July, and many of Glamorgan's home fixtures were spoilt.

Yorkshire

When tracing the county table in reverse order, one would not normally expect to come across Yorkshire so early in the search, but 1947 was their worst season since 1910 and 1911, when they were eighth and ninth. Between times they had been out of the top four only once, and that was when they were fifth in 1934. The sharing of seventh place with Worcestershire was, therefore, a calamity. It was felt the more acutely in that, to the manner born, Yorkshire had carried off the title in 1946, appearing to be picking up where they left off in 1939. But it had been, like several other sides, a troupe of ancients. Now Maurice Leyland, Cyril Turner and Wilf Barber had retired, and Arthur Booth, wracked with arthritis, was incapable of repeating his triumphs of 1946. This 44-year-old substitute for Verity could manage only four matches and took only 7 wickets.

It was his successor, the young Johnny Wardle, whose left-hand spin bemused Somerset in their first innings at Leeds, while his colleague, E. P. Robinson, was equally telling with his off-breaks in the second. Yorkshire won by an innings, but it was to be their last success in the Championship for weeks. This unhappy run began with draws against Hampshire and Middlesex. Walker, a local league player, scored 91 on his debut against Hampshire, the county who adopted him the following year, but the bowlers could not drive home the advantage. At Lord's Yorkshire had to work hard for safety, and rain on the first day was, in retrospect, a helpful factor.

There was little, if anything, to comfort their grieving supporters. At Sheffield poor fielding – an unwelcome trait in the Yorkshire make-up in 1947 – contributed to a shamefully heavy loss in a low-scoring game with Notts. The next fixture was at Leeds, and it had been designated Bill Bowes's benefit. His reward of £8,000 was a Yorkshire record, but the match itself was less heartening. It was over in two enthralling days and was watched by over 40,000 people. The Yorkshire totals were but 85 and 186, and although Bowes, his pace much reduced after three years as a PoW in Germany, and Coxon had demolished Middlesex in the first innings, and Wardle had 7 for 66 in the second, it was insufficient.

In another two-day event at Tunbridge Wells, Kent won by 57 runs: the arthritic Booth took 5 of his summer's 7 wickets in the Kent first innings, and they were tumbled out for 68 in their second, but Yorkshire could not adequately respond. Wardle took another 9 wickets in the Surrey match and G. A. Smithson hit a century, but they lost this by 5 wickets. At Hull, Yorkshire were out for 79, and, at 111 for 8 in their second innings, they were grateful to the bad weather for escaping from Kent's clutches.

This was the first of five draws, including the South African match. The others were with Nottinghamshire, Leicestershire and Lancashire, against whom Yorkshire at least had the edge. After Smithson's 98 and Robinson's 5 for 61 had severely undermined Lancashire, Yorkshire were unfortunate not to thrust home the win. In spite of the bank holiday weekend being wet, 50,000 watched this game.

So Yorkshire found themselves languishing near the foot of the table at the beginning of August. They rallied with an innings victory at Leicester, where centuries by Hutton, Yardley and Smithson were the chief contributions to a massive total of 541. But the Championship leaders, Gloucestershire, visited Bradford in belligerent mood, and they won a splendid game by 8 runs.

As the weather improved, the Yorkshire batting mended and flourished. Worcestershire were thrashed by 269 runs. A cautious 147 from Willie Watson, accompanied by livelier batting from

Sellers and Smithson, was overmuch for a timid Worcester team. There was a more thrilling win over Warwickshire by 6 runs, almost on time. Coxon, with match figures of 9 for 80, and Halliday, with 97, were the Yorkshire stars. Yorkshire's eighth and last Championship win was a trouncing of Northants by 351 runs. This was the more gladdening in so far as two youthful players were mainly responsible. Ted Lester scored a century in each innings, 126 and 142, and Ron Aspinall had match figures of 14 for 65.

There were draws with Essex and Hampshire as August ended. Batting flawlessly, Len Hutton scored 197 and 104 against Essex in a high-scoring game, while, at Bournemouth, he went one further, accumulating 270 cultured runs for the highest personal score of the season. Yardley hit a century, and, in his last Championship match, Bowes delighted everyone with 5 for 52.

Hutton, after a hesitant start, had blossomed into his finest form, ending with over 1,500 runs for Yorkshire, average 70, and 2,500 in all games, average 65. During August, at county and national level, he was challenging Edrich and Compton for the label of master-batsman. His young colleague, Lester, managed, in fact, to outstride him in the averages, with a sum of 73 from eleven innings. Yardley and Watson each had 1,000 runs, while Smithson – a 'Bevin Boy', that is, deployed in the collieries for his national service – had done well enough to be taken on the West Indies tour.

It was the traditional strength of Yorkshire which, this year, was their basic weakness, for the bowling was strangely ineffective. In his last season, Bowes did well to take 61 wickets and top the averages, but no one approached 100 wickets. Robinson, Coxon and Wardle managed 70 or so each, but they were more expensive than in 1946. Robinson, for example, had taken over 120 wickets in the previous year, at an average of 14; this year it was 77 at 21.

There were signs of future glory. Wardle had done well enough to join Smithson on the boat for the West Indies, and Aspinall showed promise as an all-rounder. The problem of the wicket-keeping berth was solved – and for many years – by the success of the amateur, D. V. Brennan, and Yardley's continuing progress was noteworthy. He was about to take over the captaincy in 1948, having already captained England with panache.

But seven losses and ten draws in the county matches was not really Yorkshire's style, and only a victory or two in the closing stages of the tournament dragged them painfully into the middle of the table. Transition was the word mostly on the lips of Yorkshire committee men – and assuredly their team was to enjoy considerable success before the horrors that befell it thirty or forty years later.

Worcestershire

Worcestershire, seventh in 1939 and eighth in 1946, were recovering from a long and mediocre run of results, yawning back to before the First World War. They shared seventh place with Yorkshire in 1947, and thereafter became a county to be reckoned with. There were to be odd spells of failure, but, generally speaking, the county was destined to do well, and eventually excellently.

In 1947 they won seven county matches, one less than Yorkshire, and lost eleven. In the main they enjoyed a fairly humdrum, pleasing, if untheatrical season.

After a victorious start to the summer, they fared badly, and, indeed, they did not win again until the second week of June. Then they beat Warwickshire at Dudley by 7 wickets. Don Kenyon virtually won the game for them single-handed with an impressive 152 not out, as Worcester paced themselves to 272 for 3, winning with a quarter of an hour remaining. It was Kenyon's first Championship century, and the first of many, as he soon developed into one of the most reliable of county batsmen. P. F. Jackson and Roly Jenkins were the pick of the bowlers. Next they beat Sussex at Horsham by 6 wickets. The pattern was not dissimilar. Bird's hundred and Jenkins's match haul of 10 for 157 established the opportunity for Kenyon and the captain, A. F. T. White, to knock off most of the runs required. Worcester scored 124 in just over an hour, winning with three minutes to spare.

After that came losses to Gloucestershire, Leicestershire and Somerset. Edwin Cooper batted well and Reg Perks took 6 for 66 against Leicester, only for Worcester to be jostled out for 80 in their second innings. Perks and Howorth bowled tidily against Somerset, but the batting was nondescript. In the return match a week later, Worcestershire were lucky to draw. After consistent batting in the first innings, and after Howorth had taken 7 for 60, they succumbed to 93 for 9 by the close.

July continued fruitlessly. Worcestershire drew with Hampshire, a game in which Cooper batted grandly and Jackson had 6 for 52, and with Glamorgan at Ebbw Vale, where Jenkins took 6 for 52, and where Worcester tried courageously to raise 259 runs in 165 minutes, ending with 215 for 7. Gloucestershire completed the double over them, winning by 65 runs, and with only Perks's 6 for 60 as consolation, while the Lancashire game at Stourbridge was spoilt by rain, and ended in another draw. More rain afflicted the Sussex match at Worcester, and that was also drawn, although not before the home side had totalled 458 for 5 declared, of which Wyatt scored a blistering 166 not out.

Eleven first-class games consecutively without a win: that was the dreary record for the middle part of the summer, and one which sent Worcestershire tumbling down the table. But suddenly it was a royal progress to four successive victories. Warwickshire were beaten by 10 wickets, Northants by 8 wickets, Essex by 10 wickets and, more narrowly, Glamorgan by 14 runs, the last Welsh wicket falling in the last over of the extra half hour. Howorth took 6 for 31 against Warwickshire; Bob Wyatt (now aged 46) had another big hundred against Northamptonshire; Perks devastated Essex with 6 for 24; and C. H. Palmer, a Bromsgrove schoolmaster, made 124 and Howorth took 6 for 45 versus Glamorgan. These were the star performances, but, in truth, the whole team batted and bowled with more regularity and precision over this time.

But that bouncy fortnight of assurance, which took the county into the top half of the table, did not last, and the season finished with a draw and four defeats. It began with a daunting experience at Wellingborough, where Northants won by 8 wickets in two days, only Howorth and Jackson emerging with any credit. The unhelpful Dudley pitch guaranteed that a drawn match would ensue with Nottinghamshire. Both Kenyon, 102, and Palmer, 177, then his highest score in county cricket, were in top-class form, while Howorth's 6 for 50 (5 for 13 in the last stage of the Nottingham innings) was masterly.

Worcestershire could do no right in the oppressive heat of August. R. T. D. Perks's benefit match versus Yorkshire hardly survived into the third day, for Worcester's partners in seventh place in the table thrashed them soundly by 269 runs. There was little to remark in the Worcester display: Perks took no wickets, and managed but a single in each innings. However, 11,000 paid on the first two days, and Perks won a pleasant reward for his years of tireless bowling. Two more rather uncompromising defeats completed Worcester's year of light and shade. Kent won at Dover by 135 runs, a display enlivened only by Jackson's steady bowling in the first innings and some obdurate batting from Jenkins in the second; and they ended their season somewhat early, on 25 August, collapsing twice, for 56 and 174, before the Derbyshire attack and losing in two days by 10 wickets.

As in 1946, Dick Howorth was the first to reach the double, a feat he achieved early in August. He scored 1,064 runs in the Championship, and took 118 wickets at a cost of just under 17 each. In all cricket he scored 1,510 runs and took 164 wickets, and it was the seventh season in a row he had reached 100 wickets. He was undoubtedly one of the successes of the year. His artful flight and searching spin belied his languid mien, and he batted with a sure correctness, so much so that his career furnished him with over 1,000 wickets and over 10,000 runs. Roly Jenkins also proved to be a useful all-rounder, his leg-breaks gaining him 55 wickets and his watchful batsmanship just short of 1,000 runs. Two other bowlers were outstanding. Reg Perks took 101 wickets, and was as persevering as ever, while Peter Jackson captured 94 wickets with his out-swingers. The bowlers were ably assisted by the wicket-keeper, Hugo Yarnold, whose 87 victims in all matches constituted a Worcestershire record.

The batting was much less sound. Don Kenyon and Edwin Cooper just reached their 1,000 runs, but others seemed to be in and out of the side, and possibly in and out of form. There was an imbalance of experience and freshness. R. E. S. Wyatt was now past his considerable best, but he scored 775 runs in fifteen games, whereas Laddie Outschoorn, from Sri Lanka, who had been imprisoned by the Japanese, was still feeling his way into the side. Palmer topped the averages with 44, but played only eight games. There was spirited batting from the skipper, A. F. T. White, but Fred Cooper and Bird did not have exciting seasons. At a time when many counties had a familiar look about the first five places in their batting order, Worcestershire were in something of a muddle. As a result, they were occasionally dismissed for low and, in such a summer, disgraceful scores. They possibly surprised themselves by finishing as high as seventh.

Surrey

One of the reasons for some of the odd placements in the table was the remarkable congestion of traffic in the middle, with several places shared and an egalitarian distribution of points. Thus the middle seven counties ranged only from 100 to 120 points, with those two totals and 116 being, in fact, the sole numbers in question. Yet they covered places seventh to thirteenth in the table. These were the teams that had won seven or eight games, usually losing as many, if not slightly more. Surrey were a cut above this ruck, if only marginally. They were the last of the big six, the counties which had won ten or more matches and had lost less than they had won. They won ten, lost seven, drew eight, and ended the season with 140 points.

Surrey had been eleventh in 1946. They had been eleventh four times before, but they had never dropped lower than that. Their record was a proud one. In the 1950s they were to be the most powerful county, to cricket what Liverpool would be to football in the 1980s – and with an exposition of some of the same careful technical application.

So much for hindsight. In the event, Surrey began and ended the season in slovenly fashion, giving rise to displeasure as well as dissatisfaction among their followers. Captained once more by E. R. T. Holmes, the beginning of June found them languishing near the foot of the table, and they lost the admirable Laurie Fishlock, sick with appendicitis, for many games. They had so far won just one match, and the whole of June was to furnish them with only one further success.

Rain and slow batting produced a barren draw in the Lancashire match at the Oval, although the up-and-coming D. G. W. Fletcher continued to show heartening form. On 12 June an entertaining one-day fixture marked the Surrey centenary. Field-Marshal

Montgomery, who was born at St Mark's vicarage hard by the Oval, was the guest of honour. Surrey made 315 for 6, the runs being generally spread among all the batsmen. The Old England side included two over-60s in Charlie Parker and J. W. Hitch, who took a couple of wickets and scored a half century. Jack O'Connor, now the Eton coach, batted adeptly for his hundred, and, at 305 for 8, Old England fell just short of the target. The enterprising wicket-keeping of George Duckworth was much admired.

More rain and more lethargy in batting led to a draw with Cambridge University at Guildford, and the second fixture of the Guildford Week, with Sussex, was also drawn: it degenerated into a struggle for first innings points, which Surrey lost. Then came June's single win when Glamorgan were defeated by an innings and 180 runs. Squires and McIntyre scored centuries, Barling was run out on 99, and Holmes weighed in with 80, as Surrey amassed 560 for 8 declared.

The bespectacled Squires was again in form at Peterborough, where Surrey were unfortunate not to complete a win over Northants. Laker had taken 6 for 55 in the first innings, and then storms saved the home side when Surrey were healthily placed at 96 for 1 towards 225 for victory. Back at the Oval, and in spite of another hundred from Squires, Gloucestershire won rather comfortably, but Surrey's visit to Bradford proved more rewarding. They won by 5 wickets, much of the credit being rightly attributed to Fletcher, who patiently carried his bat for 127, and the Bedser twins, who shared 15 wickets.

Not a ball was bowled in the Derbyshire match at Chesterfield, but the win over Yorkshire had put Surrey on their mettle, and they were launched on their most satisfying phase of the summer. The Kent match had been allocated for the joint benefit of Alf Gover and Tom Barling, and they could not have asked for a finer game of cricket. Parker's 58 steadied the county, and 280 runs were assembled. Kent replied with 258, Laker taking the last 3 wickets for 8 runs, as Kent threatened to overtake them. Parker scored a second half century, as Surrey, all out for 233, set their rivals 256 in three hours. Alec Bedser took the last 2 wickets in consecutive balls, as Surrey won a most evenly-balanced contest by 13 runs. Alf Gover had match figures of 9 for 166.

Surrey promptly completed the double over Kent, beating them at Blackheath by 6 wickets in another hard struggle. Next came another wholesome win, this time over Derbyshire. The margin was 193 runs. Driving with immense power, J. F. Parker made 204 not out and, with A. V. Bedser's match figures of 11 for 102, it was very much a two-man affair, but none the less welcome for that.

There was another win at Chelmsford, where Surrey narrowly beat Essex by 2 wickets. Despite Laker's 7 for 94, Essex seemed to have the game in control, but McIntyre, Holmes and Alec Bedser struck out aggressively in the final hour or so, and Surrey took the points. That was 1 August. It marked the end of Surrey's happy run of five wins in July: they were to win only three times more before the season's end.

Poor fielding allowed Nottinghamshire to score heavily against them at the Oval, and, although Fishlock and Squires batted soundly in the first innings, Surrey lost by 48 runs. Then they lost by 94 runs to Hampshire at Portsmouth in a thrilling game. Laker, thoroughly justifying his extended run in Surrey colours, took 8 for 69, only to see his batting comrades cede ground pitifully. Set a massive total, Surrey improved at their second attempt, Laurie Fishlock's imperturbable century giving them heart. There were only seven minutes remaining when the last Surrey batsman was out. A veil might sympathetically be drawn over Surrey's efforts to cope with their all-conquering neighbours, Middlesex, for only Squires, with 98, put up much of a fight. Attention should, however, be fixed on the gates: 54,000, comprised of 47,000 paying customers and 7,000 members, watched this fixture, and the gates were closed on the Saturday, with 30,000 packed tightly inside.

Surrey did beat Warwickshire at Coventry, where an undefeated century from Holmes and sharp bowling from Alf Gover and Alec Bedser set up a 6-wicket win. Fishlock was 96 not out in the successful victory bid. Then there were two more losses, against Glamorgan and a second at the hands of Middlesex.

However, Surrey saved the best to the last. First, they swamped Leicestershire by an innings and 201 runs. G. J. Whittaker and Jack Parker hit attractive centuries, and Squires, T. H. Clark and the Bedser twins also batted pleasingly, for a total of 576. Squires took 5 for 34 in the first and Laker 4 for 50 in the second innings, as

Leicestershire sank with hardly a trace. Second, they finished the season with a stylish win over Somerset by an innings and 73 runs. Barling and Alec Bedser scored hundreds before Somerset were twice dismissed cheaply, Gover, Alec Bedser and Laker doing most of the damage. It was a timely way to end the summer, and a joyous portent for the years ahead.

Despite the handicaps of slow pitches, dropped catches and advancing years, Gover took 109 wickets in his last season, and all told he had 1,155 victims in a cricketing life stretching back to the mid-1920s. Alec Bedser, out of sorts and out of the Test side, still managed to take 97 Championship wickets. In his best batting year he scored 612 runs and enjoyed his maiden century. Brother Eric just touched on 1,000 runs.

The experienced batsmen topped 1,000 runs as well: Parker and Squires did especially well, and Barling, nearing the end of a long career, also batted soundly. Holmes, now aged 42, reached his 1,000; Fishlock batted fluently fore and aft of the removal of his appendix; and eleven players averaged over 29. Among them was Fletcher, who, coming into the team when Fishlock was ill, played marvellously well. He was selected for the Players and for some festival cricket, and he finished the year with 1,857 first-class runs. He was to remain, neat and productive, a loyal Surrey henchman for many years, but his batting never again had quite that fresh sheen of 1947.

For those looking prospectively, it was of course the 66 wickets, average 16, of Jim Laker that was the more significant, and there is no doubt that his was the monumental debut of the summer. England lacked a forthright, orthodox off-spinner: suddenly, they had one who was soon to be regarded the best ever. He was whisked off to the West Indies for the 1947–48 tour. Apart from Laker and the two fast bowlers, there was little to boast of among the Surrey bowlers. But for those seeking omens, there was the footnote that Tony Lock played in one game, against South Africa, and took 2 for 74.

Derbyshire

Derbyshire still were able to field the nucleus of the side that had performed so staunchly in the 1930s, and which had produced the county's only title in 1936. A tumble to third from bottom in 1946 had been a major disappointment, and now the firm advance to fifth position was more like the Derbyshire of pre-war.

The Derbyshire formula of naggingly precise fast-medium bowling, supported by worthy, if seldom exhilarating, batsmanship, produced eleven wins against nine losses with one abandoned, and, a token to their attacking play, only five draws. The testimony to Derby's chief reliance on economic devastation is the low averages of Cliff Gladwin, G. H. Pope and W. H. Copson, just under 18, 19 and 20 respectively. They took 285 Championship wickets among them. On the other hand, only two batsmen scored 1,000 runs – A. F. Townsend and C. S. Elliott. T. S. Worthington was batting as elegantly as older supporters recalled from the 1930s when he was struck down by injury, and rather unceremoniously bundled out of the Derbyshire camp at the end of the summer. With 17,000 runs to his credit he is, by form and by style, one of the county's best ever half dozen batsmen. It was the more surprising because Derbyshire, one of the poorer of the counties, had scant playing resources and when players were required for Tests or lost through injury they had precious few reserves. This was to cost them dearly, for it should be remembered that, for a short while around midsummer, Derbyshire headed the table.

Having lost to Hampshire by 7 wickets during the first Test – George Pope's 6 for 61 being the only item for honourable report – Derbyshire, in fact, proceeded to win four of the next five games, with the fifth only narrowly lost. Somerset were buried in a day at Chesterfield, the first such occurrence since 1925.

Peter Vaulkhard's 84, easily his best score of the season, assisted Derbyshire nicely, but it was Pope's 13 for 50 which authentically destroyed Somerset. Curiously, he conceded 24 of those 50 runs before he took his first wicket, and then he bowled, unchanged and unchallenged, to lethal effect.

It was Pope who starred in the defeat of Sussex by 99 runs, for, after the first day had been lost through rain, he scored 61 and took 9 for 131 in the match. Worthington, with Elliott and Denis Smith in support, hit a delightful and chanceless hundred versus Leicestershire in the next match – and then Pope, savouring his excellent form, took another 10 wickets; Copson had 5 for 21 in the second innings, and Leicester went down by an innings and 105 runs.

The Lancashire match at Buxton was one of the most thrilling of a summer replete with tasty action. Cliff Gladwin took all 9 wickets to fall in a splendid spell, as Lancashire amassed 350 for 9, but Revill's maiden hundred kept Derbyshire in the hunt. Copson and Gladwin then ripped Lancashire apart, leaving only 153 needed for full points. It reached the juncture where the home team required only 6 runs with 3 wickets standing, but they muffed it, and lost by 3 runs. After making short work of a substandard Gentlemen of Ireland engagement, Derbyshire then beat Glamorgan by 4 wickets. Following a dreadful first innings display, they were set 248 in a little over 200 minutes, and they arrived at that target with ten minutes in hand. Alderman, Townsend and Vaulkhard scored the runs, whilst Gladwin had 5 for 57 in the Glamorgan first innings.

It was now July, and Derbyshire's dominant phase was behind them. They lost to Gloucestershire by 2 wickets. Denis Smith, Rhodes and Marsh saved Derbyshire in their first innings, but they fell apart at their second attempt: nonetheless, Dusty Rhodes, bowling his leg-breaks acutely, made Gloucester struggle for their win. Rain spoilt the next two matches. There was a draw with Kent, a game distinguished by the consistent batting of A. F. Townsend and by more useful bowling from Rhodes. The Surrey match saw not one ball bowled. There was a heavy defeat at the hands of Lancashire, and then Derbyshire lost to the South Africans.

They were back on the winning road at Ilkeston. It was a low-scoring and see-saw affair, with Derbyshire gaining the edge over Nottingham by 15 runs. It was another triumph for George Pope and his deadly in-swingers. His match figures were 12 for 101, and these included a hat-trick in the first innings. Derbyshire were rather mauled at the Oval, for, despite a Townsend hundred, Surrey were always able to score too heavily for Derbyshire tastes.

The switchback continued. First there was a win at Rushden by 7 wickets. Northants held their own in the first exchanges, but all was altered by an amazing spell of 8 for 26 from Gladwin. Then there was a defeat by Leicestershire: centuries by J. D. Eggar, the old

Oxford Blue who was able to join the side in August, and by George Pope, plus the sly leg-breaks of Rhodes, had set up an entertaining finale. Leicester needed a daunting 391 and, after early shocks, they just managed to prevail in the very last over. Strong all-round batting and the destructive bowling of Pope and Gladwin forced Warwickshire to follow on, but Derbyshire could not press home the advantage, and this match was drawn.

Essex beat Derbyshire by 5 wickets, and next came two draws. One was with Nottinghamshire, and was highlighted by Eggar, with 173, and Charlie Elliott, with 215, joining in a stand of 349 for the second wicket, the largest ever Derbyshire partnership. The other was at Scarborough, where, on a docile wicket, scoring was plentiful, especially by Yorkshire. Townsend's 137 and Pope's 90, along with steadfast batting in the second innings, averted any chance of defeat, and Rhodes trundled diligently away for 8 for 162 in 46 overs.

There was a tough battle to follow with Hampshire, but this game Derbyshire won by 68 runs. Not unexpectedly, the county were routed by Middlesex, only Eggar and Pope doing much by way of counterattack with the bat. What bemused and astonished the sporting world was the hat-trick performed by the Derbyshire skipper, E. J. Gothard, who had previously taken only 1 first-class wicket. He took 18 wickets in his entire career for Derbyshire, and, as he scored only about 500 runs, it must be confessed he was very much in the 'non-playing' tradition of captaincy. That said, he led with vim, as he exemplified in the last match of the summer, when Worcestershire were roundly beaten inside two days.

Denis Smith, who had undertaken the wicket-keeping and who had also suffered from injury, had, by his own standards, a slightly disappointing year, just as Rhodes had mixed unplayable with eccentric bouts of leg-break bowling. What with these minor problems and the comings and going of one or two amateurs, Derbyshire had seemed to be a team over-dependent on three quick bowlers and three or four competent batsmen. Above all and, let it be noted, in a summer renowned for the eloquence of its batsmanship, it was the uncompromising, niggling accuracy and sting of Gladwin, Pope and Copson which brought decent rewards to Derbyshire in 1947.

Kent

How impeccably Kent upheld the traditional conventions of the hallowed county ideal! Their pastoral grounds and sporting attitudes contributed to this Corinthian scene, and in men like Lord Harris and Frank Woolley they had respectively interpreted the most excellent attributes of undiluted amateurism and urbane professionalism. Popular legend then had it that the Kentish county cap was the most difficult to win and that deportment and manners were a weighty part of the assessment. Although they had three times won the Championship in the Edwardian era, it seemed almost philistine for these representations of cricketing aestheticism to be so avidly ambitious. To be fourth, as in 1947, had about it a certain sense of propriety and correctness. It was the kind of position – high, but not o'er-vaunting – that Kent normally kept. Alas, 1947 was to mark the end of that lengthy and civilised history. Kent was perhaps the first of the great counties to suffer the gross effects of modernism, for they sank to fifteenth in 1948 (their worst since the tragic year of 1895, when they were unaccountably last in the pre-expanded competition) and never quite came to terms with modern times until the late 1960s.

They began 1947 in tremendous heart, pushing near the head of the table as June unfolded. They drew with Nottinghamshire at Gravesend among high scoring, some rain and a rash of dropped catches. Les Ames mastered the Nottingham attack completely, with 212 and 53, both undefeated. He continued to enjoy the Gravesend air, scoring another hundred against Northants. Leslie Todd also hit a century, and Hearn and Fagg were among the runs. Doug Wright took 11 wickets, as Kent won by 9 wickets. There was a 52-run victory at the expense of Leicestershire, for, at rainy Loughborough, the experience of Fagg and a blistering display by Wright –12 for 107 – was much too much for the home side.

Suddenly, there was a disconcerting lapse in form, and Kent went down four times with a bump. First, Nottinghamshire beat them by an innings, only a fine century from Ames and two punchy knocks by Godfrey Evans seeming temporarily to stem the tide. Second, Gloucestershire won by a similar margin. Third, Glamorgan also won, by an innings yet again; once more Ames was the batting star, but again, as a team performance, it was woeful. Fourth, on returning home to Tunbridge Wells, Sussex beat them by 6 wickets.

Tunbridge Wells was also the arena for an astonishing fixture with Yorkshire. Although shot out for an impoverished 68 in their second innings, Kent's varied attack of Harding, Wright and Dovey twice thwarted the Yorkshiremen, who eventually lost in two days by 57 runs. In spite of this boost to morale, Kent then went another five games without a win, and they were sliding ominously down the table.

They drew with Derbyshire at Dore, not much used for first-class cricket; and with Yorkshire at Hull, another site little visited by first-class cricketers. The weather played havoc with both matches, but Kent were unlucky not to complete the double over Yorkshire. Next there were two defeats. One was against Surrey, as Kent's mid-July tour continued, but by only 13 runs, and the other was against Warwickshire, by a mere 6 runs. Then Surrey won the return fixture at Blackheath by 6 wickets. Fagg and Davies batted soundly and Wright once more had a good haul, but it was to no avail.

It was nearly the end of July, and Kent had won only one of their last ten games. Ames, suffering from a strain, had been ruefully missed for several games, and there had been occasional Test calls, but beyond excuses Kent could point to a number of matches only narrowly lost or drawn. There was no material need for chagrin, and Kent now proceeded to remain undefeated by another county for the rest of the summer, and they soared up the table again.

Somerset were the first to feel the weight of the rejuvenated Kent, losing by 7 wickets at Maidstone. A Todd century and doughty out-cricket paid dividends. The second Maidstone game was a high-scoring draw with Essex. All the Kentish batsmen took advantage of the balmy conditions, not least Todd and Ames, who both scored centuries. Canterbury was the venue for Todd's benefit, and that worthy was in fine fettle. He scored 68 against Hampshire, while Fagg's hundred, Wright's 10 wickets and strong support from Ames and Valentine enabled Kent to overwhelm them by an innings in two days. Although the third day was lost, the general attraction of Kent cricket and the improvement in the weather meant that Todd enjoyed a generous benefit. Over 13,000 paid admission on the bank holiday Monday.

Middlesex were the next visitors to Canterbury. Fagg obliged with his second century of the festival, and Wright's 6 for 87 ensured that Middlesex, unusually, had to follow on. Their second endeavour was more characteristic, and they eventually set Kent the fearful target of 232 in two hours. Valentine and Pawson cracked 95 in a little over half an hour, and 181 for 6 at the close reflected credit on both sides. Middlesex bowled 48 overs in that two hour session.

Sussex were defeated by 9 wickets. Fagg continued his form with 163 and 59 not out, and Wright, at his disconcerting best, took 15 for 173, including a hat-trick that forced Sussex to follow on. Then came Kent's premier display of the year. At a juncture when the Championship was causing much excitement, they beat Middlesex at Lord's with five minutes to spare. The formula was the same: free and regular scoring underpinned by Wright's glittering assaults. This time he took 11 for 194. Kent's last two home fixtures were at Dover, and both ended in very convincing wins. Todd and Ames hit centuries in yet another large total, and Ridgway took 10 wickets in this 251-run rout of Leicestershire. Worcestershire were easily beaten as well, by 135 runs. At Taunton, winning the toss for the twelfth successive time, Kent scored freely, with Todd making 173 and sharing a large opening partnership with Arthur Fagg. Wright, exhibiting his adroitness on a placid pitch, had 7 more victims, but Somerset clung stubbornly to the mast of a draw on the last day. Finally, Kent lost to the South Africans at Canterbury in a match of brisk run-making.

Such a summary of Kent's activities must clearly demonstrate the competence of the county's three leading professional batsmen. Ames, 2,137 runs, average 71; Todd, 2,000, average 45; Fagg, 1,947, average 43: these were the men and the figures on which Kent's success was founded. The captain, Brian Valentine, scored his 1,000 runs, and ensured that Kent almost always attacked, as twelve wins and only six draws testify. It is equally apparent that Douglas Wright was by far the most successful bowler. He had 138 county wickets, and 177 in all first-class cricket, the second best tally of the summer. His county average was 18.5, straining credulity, given the normal expense of leg-break bowling. Dovey, the off-spinner, and the two quicker men, Ridgway and Harding, lent commendable, but rarely authoritative, assistance, and J. G. W. Davies fielded brilliantly as well as offering useful help with bat and ball. (In parenthesis, it should be sorrowfully noted that all Kent cricket lovers were to be shocked by Harding's death that autumn from infantile paralysis.)

Kent had played marvellously dazzling cricket, and the crowds had responded as wonderfully. Over 182,000 paid at the gates, double the numbers for 1939, a quarter of them through the juvenile turnstiles, while the Canterbury festival alone attracted close on 50,000 spectators. Naturally, these statistics do not include the thousands of visits paid to these games by members and their friends. The more thoughtful of these visitors may have pondered on the fact that Kent, for all their bright and popular appeal, depended mainly on four accomplished professionals of a pre-war vintage. The county's future prospects were less vividly pronounced. The one major exception, of course, was Godfrey Evans. He kept wicket with unparalleled skill. His season's haul was 67 catches and 25 stumpings, and he would reign supreme behind the stumps for Kent and England for years to come.

Lancashire

Unduly ravaged by the passing of the war years, Lancashire had still managed to assemble a no-nonsense squad of artisan craftsmen, several of them well versed in the sometimes enervating trade of the county circuit. It was a balanced team, fitted for most occasions, and above all it was difficult to beat. They lost just once, and that to Somerset, whereas Gloucestershire lost four and Middlesex five times. Conversely, they drew as many as ten, leaving themselves, with 13 wins and a tie, 20 points behind Gloucestershire.

Cyril Washbrook and Winston Place were the premier opening pair among the counties in 1947. Washbrook, tough, aggressive, cocksure, scored over 1,600 runs (average 78) in the Championship, and 2,662 in all, for an average of 68. Of the major batsman, he was third only to Compton and Edrich – and Place, more contemplative, perhaps, but technically just as adept, was only a whisker behind.

His figures were 2,501 (average 63), almost all of his runs coming in the Championship. With J. T. Ikin, despite illness and injury, and G. A. Edrich, tenacious and willing, also scoring 1,000 runs, and with Kenneth Cranston not far off that yearned-for mark, the batting was always capable and regular in its production of the necessary runs.

Dick Pollard, locally worshipped as 'th'owd chain-'orse', bowled his customary 1,200 overs with authentic and unremitting zeal. His 144 wickets were just pickings, and only Alec Bedser among the quicker bowlers completed so much work. He was abetted by W. B. Roberts, the left-hander, orthodox to the point of piety, who took 81 first-class wickets. With W. E. Phillipson far below his best, the value of Cranston, who had 56 county victims, and of Ikin, who had 48, was plain to see. But there were useful reserves in attack and defence – Alan Wharton, the young brothers Nigel and Barry Howard, J. B. Bowes, R. G. Garlick and Eric Price, for instance – so that Lancashire were rarely at a loss. If anything, it was Cranston's rather green approach to captaincy and the lack of a top-grade wicket-keeper (something that would haunt Lancashire until the arrival of Farokh Engineer) that were the weaknesses.

Lancashire had been third in 1946, and with just a tremble in 1949, they were to perform with the same stolid constancy for a number of years, including their half share of the Championship in 1950. However, their mainstays were the tyros of the 1930s, and, although Statham and Tattersall would provide class in attack, this good Lancashire side gradually disintegrated, and from 1960 Lancashire cricket was to undergo something of a nightmare.

June 1947 found them in dour form, the pattern of wins and draws having already been laid. They drew with Surrey at the Oval in a dreary and rain-affected match, in which Place scored a cautious century; and they drew with Glamorgan at Liverpool, after rational all-round play had left their opponents in what should have been a hopeless impasse. This inability to polish off reeling opposition was next exemplified in another game marred by the weather. After a commanding century by Washbrook, Essex staved off what might have been a heavy defeat. Washbrook scored his fourth consecutive century at Old Trafford – he scored nine for Lancashire in 1947 – as Cambridge University were accounted for, Cranston being the leading wicket-taker.

In a topsy-turvy game at Buxton, Lancashire, so triumphal in their first innings and so abject in their second, barely managed to beat Derbyshire by 3 runs, but this excitement, mixed with relief, was soon displaced by frustration. Howard's maiden century, 124 from Geoff Edrich, and 6 for 32 from Pollard left Warwickshire punch-drunk, but the rains visited the holiday resort of Blackpool as only 2 wickets remained for the taking. Edrich and Pollard were again the most successful in another fine team display which easily disposed of Leicestershire, and, moving directly from Manchester to Melton Mowbray, Lancashire completed the double over them. Ikin enjoyed his first Championship hundred and Roberts and Pollard did most of the bowling in this 10-wicket victory.

The county drew with Nottinghamshire in a very high-scoring encounter, during which Place scored one of his ten centuries of the summer; and with Warwickshire, a match that might have been won save for rain. Place, recently in superb form, scored 135 and Pollard took 6 for 77. Derbyshire were not so lucky back at Old Trafford, for they fell grievously by an innings and 93 runs. Pollard then weighed in with an apt and sterling 8 for 33 against Northants – his best-ever bowling – and Lancashire won by 8 wickets. Place and Barry Howard made centuries.

As a consequence of the cheerless weather, the away games with Worcestershire and Glamorgan were drawn. Lancashire caved in to Somerset in lacklustre fashion for their solitary loss of the season. Over August bank holiday at Sheffield there was another poor and anonymous display, and the county were fortunate not to add a second defeat immediately after the Somerset débâcle.

Whether these lapses jolted them into sharper action, or whether the harder wickets of August suited them better, is difficult to judge. Whatever the reason, they won six of their last eight matches, and ended a comfortable third in the table. The odd two games were a drawn encounter with South Africa and that exciting tie at Bournemouth with Hampshire. Cranston's 155 not out, early on, had given Lancashire every chance, but after a fine start from Place and from Washbrook, who hit a rapid hundred, Lancashire, needing 1 run off the last over, lost their last wicket in a run-out.

That clears the decks to study Lancashire's excellent sequence of six victories. The first was over Gloucestershire, challenging hard for the title, and this 10-wicket victory owed much to the bowling of Pollard and Cranston, and to yet another great opening stand – this time of 183 – by the old firm of Washbrook and Place. Place then scored 171 at Clacton versus Essex, while Geoff Edrich compiled a lively 132. Essex were faced with 510 and, with Cranston taking 8 wickets in the match, they were swept aside by an innings. Place did even better against Nottingham, who were beaten by 84 runs. He scored a century in each innings, and was thoroughly to deserve his trip to the West Indies as one of the MCC tourists. Ikin's 11 for 119 comprised the best bowling of his career. Next, Hampshire were outclassed. Lancashire won in a canter by an innings and 80 runs. Geoff Edrich and John Ikin provided the runs, and Pollard destroyed the first Hampshire attempt with 6 for 23.

Lancashire finished their rewarding summer with a southern jaunt, which included the Hampshire tie. Sussex must have been very tired of the sight of Washbrook and Place, who, it will be recalled, had put them to the sword earlier in the season. Now Washbrook scored 176, and, when in the second innings Lancashire were asked to reach 233 in two hours, the intrepid pair hit a hundred each, and Lancashire won with ten minutes to spare. It is worth remarking that Sussex bowled 42 overs in those 110 torrid minutes. Finally and proudly, Lancashire beat the champions on their own territory. The consistent batting of the first innings was typical of Lancashire's whole approach, and they backed this with sound fielding and tidy bowling. Eric Price and Ikin shared 15 wickets. It was a commendable, as well as a characteristic, end to their summer.

Gloucestershire

Fortified by the Graces, Gloucestershire had enjoyed successes during what some might view as the medieval history of the County Championship. Since then, they had had to settle for mid-table positions, although the 1930s – the Hammond years – had found them pushing nearer the head of the league. Longer in the tooth, and wiser in the lore of cricket, many of the same players emerged unscathed from the war, and gave Gloucestershire a familiar and confident look. Fifth in 1946, they proceeded to give Middlesex a brisk run for their money, eventually finshing twenty points behind them, having won seventeen games, lost four and drawn five. Although they have since been second or third on only a tiny handful of occasions, this was to be almost as close to the title as they have ever approached, excepting in those far off years of W. G. Grace.

By June, and having dismissed from their minds the wretched reverse at Lord's at the beginning of the season, Gloucestershire had embarked on winning ways, and it would be early August before they suffered their next defeat. The spin partnership of Goddard and Cook was already established as one of the ornaments of a decorous summer. Goddard took 15 for 134 against Leicestershire, as those worthies lost by 6 wickets. Barnett scored a dogged 228 in this match. There were draws with Warwickshire and Glamorgan. In the former game, and in spite of a further 11 victims for Goddard, and a patient century by W. L. Neale, they were lucky to survive, but A. E. Wilson's rearguard action sufficed. In the latter fixture, the boot was on the other foot, for Goddard and Cook dismissed Glamorgan for 90 in their first innings, and only valiant defence kept Gloucestershire at bay.

Then they beat Worcestershire by 6 wickets in an even-handed contest, in which Sam Cook and J. F. Crapp shone. The powerful Kent side came badly unstuck at Bristol. Crapp and Emmett scored hundreds as the home team rattled up 507, and Goddard's match figures of 10 for 170 completed the story. There was a drawn match at Trent Bridge, where Nottinghamshire had much the best of it; only a thunderstorm rescued Gloucestershire. Down, next, to the Oval, where the county rallied and beat Surrey by 8 wickets. Immensely consistent batting was the base, while Goddard's 11 wickets included his 100th of the season; unsurprisingly, he was the first bowler to reach that target. In a boisterous finale, they scored 47 in 22 minutes, leaving only three minutes in hand.

There was a close encounter with Derbyshire, which Gloucestershire managed to win by 2 wickets. C. J. Barnett, Crapp and the captain, B. O. Allen, were the chief contributors to that narrow victory. Rain spoilt the Sussex match, which quickly deteriorated into a tedious draw, but Worcestershire were beaten by 65 runs after they had put Gloucestershire in. Goddard's well-nigh unplayable off-breaks – he had match figures of 11 for 120 – turned the scale. With Sam Cook in tandem, he wrought havoc in match after match. They next took 9 wickets apiece as Northants fell apart, losing by 84 runs. Having beaten the Combined Services with some ease, Gloucestershire next overpowered Somerset. Only two days of the August holiday weekend were required, for Somerset collapsed for 98 and 25, giving Gloucestershire a resounding 316 runs victory. On the Monday of that rout, a large crowd of over 12,000 was in attendance. Goddard had 7 for 61, and, incredibly, 5 for 4 including the hat-trick. The Bristol square had been subjected to scientific research and a generous application of sand, and this made it very helpful to spin bowlers. Few teams came to terms with Goddard and his accomplice, Cook, in those circumstances.

It was time for a trip to the north, and time for a rare loss. This was at Manchester, where, after a hundred from Crapp and 6 more wickets for Tom Goddard, Gloucestershire did badly in their second innings. Across to Bradford, where Yorkshire were beaten by 8 runs: Emmett's century and the accurate bowling of Lambert, Cook and, of course, Goddard saw Gloucestershire home in an absorbing finish.

The Cheltenham festival began with an undistinguished performance against the South Africans. This was scarcely the right preparation for the clash with Middlesex, with only four points separating the sides. Middlesex won by 68 runs, of which a little more anon: one might at this juncture notice the record crowd of 14,500 and the closed gates for the Saturday. The third match of the series ended in a win over Glamorgan. It was a low-scoring affair, in which Barnett and Wilson batted well, but in which the main honours again went to Cook (6 for 56 in the first innings) and Goddard (8 for 61 in the second).

Although there were two or three matches remaining, all but the constitutionally mathematical regarded the matter of the Championship as closed by the Cheltenham fixture with Middlesex. That had been what in footballing circles is known as a 'four- or six-pointer'. In any event, Gloucestershire had mixed fortunes as August ended. After the Glamorgan victory, they drew with Hampshire and lost to Sussex. At Bournemouth, the batsmen were in total authority: Basil Allen hit a polished 220, and Crapp a masterly 131. Wilson and Crapp batted in fresh and vigorous style at Hove, but the team seemed impatient and a little nervous, and Hove in late August was no place for spin attacks. Sussex won comfortably, and any slight remaining hopes of the title vanished.

However, Gloucestershire completed their itinerary in an attractive manner, in decent keeping with their season's exploits. Two big scores, the result of typically consistent batting, coupled with, as the perfect coda to their prolific summer, no less than 19 wickets for Goddard and Cook: it was all too overwhelming for Essex, who succumbed by 317 runs. Gloucestershire, having led the table through July and into the middle of August, were meritorious runners-up, twenty points behind the triumphant Middlesex.

There was no secret about Gloucestershire's success. It revolved around the lethal combine of Goddard and Cook, and whilst their arts might have been arcane, the results, especially on the frequently favourable wickets, were evident enough. Now almost 47, Tom Goddard had doubled in his cunning and never slackened in his martial attitudes over his long career. In temper more reminiscent of the pace bowler, he utilised his venomous off-breaks with destructive effect. He took 206 wickets (average 16) for the county, and 238 (average 17, second only to John Clay in the leading national averages) in all. He bowled nearly 1,500 overs, and no one approached his huge haul of victims. It was a nonpareil display for a veteran in a season devoted chiefly to the breakage of batting records, and it must be assessed as a phenomenon not much less amazing than the Compton/Edrich one. With nearly 3,000 first-class wickets, he stands a proud fifth in the ranks of world wicket-takers – and yet he played only eight times for England.

Sam Cook, young, skilful and convivial, was his protégé and assistant executioner, and he took 120 county wickets. Between them, they capturd 326 of the 456 Championship wickets to fall to Gloucester bowlers. Barnett and Lambert were responsible for the quicker bowling, but this was usually no more than preface to the spin bowling chapters.

The batting was sound and balanced in type. Charles Barnett, never quite at his formidable best; Jack Crapp; the adaptable George Emmett; Andy Wilson, one of the best wicket-keeper-batsmen in the country; and B. O. Allen all mustered 1,000 runs, without any of them levitating in the magical cricketing way that half a dozen batsmen did that summer. Allen exhorted his players and ensured they were a reasonable fielding outfit and, all in all, it was an impressive season. Gloucestershire members might have been forgiven for musing that, had Walter Hammond been fit and willing to contribute another season of his prime form, then the Championship would have been theirs.

Middlesex

Save for a roughish spell in the early 1930s and for those occasional maverick seasons which sully the record of the best-regulated clubs, Middlesex have been one of the most regularly successful counties. Their immediately previous history was most remarkable. They had been second in the four years preceding the war, and they were second again in 1946. They seized the opportunity caused by the abrupt disintegration of Yorkshire in 1947 and grasped the title avidly. They were to be third in 1948 and first again in 1949. After this, they were to take a back seat until, following a lengthy dearth, they won the Championship in 1976 and continued in promising vein until the present. Nonetheless, there were not to be many years when they were entirely engulfed in mediocrity.

This was indeed their finest hour: they won the title in the year said by many to be the *annus mirabilis* of the County Championship; and it was the dazzling style of their charge to victory which, more than anything, permits that uncompromising argument to be pressed. The Championship has rarely been won with such a brilliant pageant of joyous and graceful cricket as it was in 1947.

The coming of the first Test set Middlesex an intriguing poser. Would the county preserve their capacity and thirst for success without the maestros Edrich and Compton? The answer was a 3-wicket victory over Glamorgan, the spin of J. A. Young and the pace of Laurie Gray bringing them 7 wickets each, respectively, in the two Glamorgan innings. Then, at Lord's, Robertson and Brown scored 310 in a little over 200 minutes to break the Middlesex record for an opening stand and to break the resolve of their opponents, Nottinghamshire. That made seven victories in a row, but there followed a drawn game with Yorkshire. Rain

Rain interfered with the progress of Middlesex, although they easily gained the first innings points. Brown and Robertson were again in tip-top form, adding 222 for the first wicket and both hitting hundreds.

Middlesex then embarked on a long tour, which lasted over a month. They lost, with something of a reserve side, to Oxford University, but then suffered the setback of a defeat in the county competition. Essex beat them by 10 wickets. Despite the continued good form of their openers – Robertson helped himself to another hundred – Middlesex on this occasion did look a trifle brittle without their Test stars. There was immediate compensation in three convincing victories. Yorkshire were beaten by 87 runs in a match that lasted but two days. It was distinguished by the gritty accomplishments of Bill Edrich, whose 70 and 102 outclassed all other endeavours. Young took 9 wickets and Denis Compton 7 on the rain-damaged Leeds pitch. Although Hampshire, in the next match, held their own in the opening clashes, they collapsed for 78 at their second attempt, and Middlesex had a comfortable margin of 105 runs. Young had match figures of 9 for 47.

The Leicestershire match enjoyed a finale that epitomised 1947. Edrich, with 257, and Compton, with 151, were the main, if predictable, contributors to a huge total of over 600. At lunch time on the third day the home team had lost only 4 second-innings wickets, and only 80 minutes remained. With Compton taking 5 wickets (following Jim Sims's 6 in the first) Leicestershire were suddenly tumbled out – but it left Middlesex needing 66 in 25 minutes. Compton and Edrich smashed their way to an astounding victory in seven overs, with four minutes to spare. Heady stuff, indeed. Even the most spectacular limited overs matches of the modern era compare ill with such adventures.

The tour finished with an unlikely defeat at Taunton, and Somerset were proving to be a *bête-noir* for Middlesex. Representative calls and injury weakened Middlesex, and at one point Leslie Compton alternated opening the bowling with wicket-keeping. What was typical of the attitude of their captain, R. W. V. Robins, was the Middlesex essay at the 369 runs required to win, when a simple draw was the softer option. They lost by only 24 runs, and the former Haileybury skipper, Alan Fairbairn, scored a hundred.

Returning to Lord's toward the end of July, Middlesex defeated Essex in a match of tall scores. Robertson and Compton hit centuries, and everyone else chimed in with good scores, in a victory by 102 runs. Nearly 1,400 runs were amassed in the three days. Off on their travels again, Middlesex won four and drew one of a short tour of five matches. The Northants match only just struggled into the third day, as Edrich made 267, the highest score of his career, and Compton not only scored a century but took 9 wickets. Over August bank holiday at Hove, Sussex were on the receiving end of more batting assaults. Robertson and Compton hundreds and 6 for 83 from Sims brought about a forthright 9-wicket victory. Robertson and Edrich added 87 in three-quarters of an hour to win the match. There was a well-fought draw at Canterbury, where, lashed by the indignity of the follow-on, Robertson and Edrich scored hundreds to set Kent a near impossible second innings target. Compton hit one of his many centuries in the Middlesex first innings. Then Surrey were thrashed at the Oval, doubtless to the noisy satisfaction of all Middlesex fans. Brown, 98; Robertson, 127; Edrich, 157 not out; Compton, 137 not out: that meant that the towering score of 537 for 2 faced the Surrey batsmen – and, rubbing salt in the wound, Compton finished with match figures of 12 for 174. Brown and Robertson opened with 211, before the Middlesex destroyers added 287 in less than three hours.

With Test and representative calls on Lord's during the middle of the season, there was just time for one home game before Middlesex were forced on to the mercies of the railways yet once more. The match, with Kent, proved to be most exciting, and Kent won by 75 runs. Robertson hit his fifth hundred in successive games, but for once Middlesex were out-batted. Compton, with a magnificent rearguard effort of 168, did excellently, but Kent managed to uproot the last Middlesex wicket with just a few minutes left.

Gloucestershire's fine progress, and this unexpected loss, set up a match of theatrical character at Cheltenham, where Gloucestershire welcomed Middlesex to a tourney of crucial proportions. With twenty-one fixtures completed, the home team led the table by a mere four points. The only disappointment was that this game clashed with the fifth Test, and Middlesex were robbed of the services of Robertson and Compton – Edrich was unfit for Test duty, but was played by Middlesex as a batsman only. In a mood prescient of the fervour of one-day cricket finals, there were coaches of supporters ferried to the College ground, which was eventually closed with a record 14,500 inside and restive hundreds outside.

Perhaps Gloucestershire were a little late in introducing their spinners, for Edrich's 50, much of it taken off the early convention of medium pace, proved to be the top score of the match. Goddard took 7 for 70, and Middlesex were all out for 180 before tea. Jack Young opened the bowling, as he sometimes did, with his lowish trajectory, and Jim Sims soon joined in with his leg-breaks. Emmett and Crapp delayed Middlesex by stern defence, but Sims took 6 and Young 4 wickets, leaving Gloucestershire 27 runs adrift. Edrich was immediately out before the end of Saturday's play, and another large crowd was in attendance for Monday's enthralling action.

It was again a day of unbroken tension and burning sunshine. Harry Sharp, playing in his first match of the season, and Robins contributed most of the Middlesex score of 141. Whilst Sam Cook bowled an economic length at one end, Tom Goddard teased out 8 wickets at the other, but Gloucestershire were set a target of 169. Young, with 5 wickets, and Sharp, with 3 in seven balls, ensured the game did not survive the second day. Only Jack Crapp mustered any strength of resistance, and Middlesex won by 68 runs. Although the match had swung this way and that, one might judge, in retrospect, that Middlesex never quite ceded the edge they gained from the impetus of a goodish opening stand in the first hour of Saturday.

That battle of the titans was justly felt to be the crux of the Championship, and so it was to prove. Nonetheless, Middlesex had to go on winning to endorse that assessment. They swamped Derbyshire by 212 runs, with runs galore from Brown – 95 and 150 not out – and Leslie Compton's maiden century. Young took 6 for 28 in the Derby first innings. They ran up 462 against Surrey, Denis Compton and F. G. Mann adding 304 in just over 200 minutes, and won by 8 wickets. Ian Bedford, the young leg-spinner, took 5 for 53 during Surrey's first efforts. Then they made absolutely certain of the title with a devastating rout of Northants inside two days. This time the bowlers were to the fore in helpful conditions. Northants lost by 355 runs, having been twice demolished by Young and Sims, who took 18 wickets between them. Middlesex lost to a resolute Lancashire side by 64 runs, but not before Compton had notched his sixteenth century of the summer, thus equalling Jack Hobbs's record.

Middlesex drew only two county matches, and of the five they lost, three occurred when large totals were being attempted in short spaces of time. They won nineteen and, in so doing, they passed the 400 mark eleven times and declared twenty times. The bowlers did sufficiently well, particularly the spin attack, for both Young and Sims gathered 100 wickets. Gray took 84 Championship wickets, but the extra bonus for Middlesex was the bowling of their great batsmen: Edrich took 47 and Compton 57 wickets. The fielding was keen, and, above all, the zealous and enterprising leadership of Robins was outstanding.

However, it was, of course, the early batting that created this celebrated triumph. The received wisdom is that Championships are normally won by superb bowling, but Middlesex won the title by the glorious expedient of scoring many runs rapidly, thereby allowing competent bowlers the time and scope to whittle away at the enemy. Not since the spacious days of 1904, when Lancashire, with J. T. Tyldesley, Reggie Spooner and Archie MacLaren in majestic flow, were champions, had a team so dominated by the authority of its batting. J. D. Robertson, handsome of mien and stroke, and S. M. Brown, pugnacious rather than stylish, constructed the platform. In all matches, they scored 2,760 and 2,078 runs respectively, sums which, in most years, would have attracted the kind of adulation poured out on the 'twins'. Building on these solid foundations, Compton scored 3,816 runs, averaging 91, and Edrich 3,539, at an average of 80. Compton's eventual eighteen centuries beat Hobbs's record, and both of these supreme virtuosi broke Tom Hayward's record of 3,518 for a season's aggregate, and that had stood since 1906. This talented quartet scored over 8,000 runs for Middlesex in 1947, and scored 33 of the 37 centuries accrued – no other Middlesex batsman reached 1,000 runs.

So did two matchless geniuses, abetted by two highly talented henchmen, seize the county competition of 1947 and shape it to their bidding.

County Championship 1947: Final Positions

	Pld.	Won	Lost	Drawn	1st Inns.	Pts.
1. Middlesex	26	19	5	2	2	236
2. Gloucestershire	26	17	4	5	3	216
3. Lancashire	26	13	1	12	6	186
4. Kent	26	12	8	6	7	172
5. Derbyshire	26	11	9	6	7	160
6. Surrey	26	10	7	9	5	140
7. Worcestershire	26	7	11	8	9	120
7. Yorkshire	26	8	7	11	6	120
9. Glamorgan	26	8	8	10	5	116
9. Sussex	26	9	12	5	2	116
11. Essex	26	6	9	11	5	100
11. Nottinghamshire	26	6	6	14	7	100
11. Somerset	26	8	12	6	1	100
14. Leicestershire	26	6	14	6	5	92
15. Warwickshire	26	6	12	8	3	84
16. Hampshire	26	4	11	11	6	78
17. Northamptonshire	26	2	16	8	6	54

The drawn games included two ties and six 'no decision' games, that is, where not even first innings points were won. A win was worth twelve and a tie six points. Four points were awarded to sides losing or drawing who had enjoyed a first innings lead. The two ties were Lancashire versus Hampshire, and Essex versus Northamptonshire.

6

Retrospect

Thus did the seventeen counties battle through that long-drawn summer. Looking through the lens of each club and its supporters, one may recall the twists and turns, the passions and the regrets, of each county, as they slowly wound their way through the intricate mesh of this competition. It is often said that the first division of the English Football League is the most gruelling of sports contests, but the County Championship cannot be far behind, in terms of its fatiguing hardship. It is apparent from a study of the fixtures that, apart from the sheer slog of the games themselves, they took place in all weathers, from the gusty chilliness of May winds, through the sodden moistness of the early summer, to the cauldron of a fierce August.

As one follows the undulating progress of one's favourites through twenty-six county fixtures and a handful of other first-class games, the additional burden of travel and overnight stays should be remembered. With motor-car travel still not widespread, most of the journeys were by rail, and they were not always comfortable. The railways had suffered badly in the war. They had operated half a million special military trains, and had been subjected to nearly 10,000 bombing incidents – 400 railwaymen had been killed and 2,444 injured by enemy action. The subsequent damage and staff shortages, coupled with the abnormal stress on and inadequate maintenance of the network, had left the railways in a dilapidated condition. On 6 August – as Arthur Fagg was scoring his immaculate 184 against Middlesex at Canterbury – the Transport Act was passed by Parliament, and this officially nationalised the rail industry. It was scarcely an ideological decision: most agreed that, without government organisation and support, the railways might well collapse. British Railways, as British Rail was first titled, started business on 1 January 1948.

Consider, then, the midsummer odyssey of Middlesex, at a crucial time when they were overhauled by Gloucestershire, who then ran neck and neck with them, until that critical Cheltenham game. Having drawn with Yorkshire at Lord's, they had to be in Oxford next day on Wednesday 18 June to play the University. They next had to transfer to Colchester for the Essex fixture on Saturday 21 June, before travelling north to Leeds for the Yorkshire return match on 28 June. They saved a day there, because of their two-days success, and had further respite, for they had a blank slot. However, they were soon boarding the old steam trains once more, across to Portsmouth to play Hampshire on Saturday 5 July, up to Leicester the following Saturday, back down to Taunton for the Somerset match on the Tuesday night, before returning to London for a home match with Essex on Saturday 19 July.

This ceaseless criss-crossing of the tracks was intermingled with accommodation which also showed the wear and tear of war, and meals which testified to the general malaise of food shortages and rationing. However biddable and hospitable people were, there was no escaping the shabbiness of some of the travel and the shoddiness of some of the billets. So, as one scrutinises the batting of Hardstaff or the bowling of Goddard, it is fair to take time to reflect that each link in the countless chain of county matches was soldered by boring waits on stations, slow, perhaps crowded, journeys, and making shift with run-down second-class hotels.

As for the cricket itself, the switchback of a county's ups and downs throughout a season reveals, at least for 1947, that there was considerable drama, and that, it appears, every day witnessed a personal act of derring-do or a concerted team performance of admirable merit. Even downtrodden Northamptonshire had their moments of genuine worth and pleasure. There is a darker side, a certain amount of dross. In part because of the weather, in part because of the inhibition of struggling for first-innings points, in part because cricket does occasionally create circumstances of tedium, there were, without doubt, periods of longueur.

In the event, the episodic dramatics of the Test matches and the winding series of county fixtures did not complete the tale of cricket in 1947. Reference has been made in passing to the doings of the universities, and both had pleasing years. Oxford won five and lost two of their twelve first-class games, and their captain, Martin Donnelly, had an outstanding summer, averaging 67 for the university and ending eighth in the main national averages. He was well supported by Pawson and W. G. Keighley, later to become one of the very few Yorkshire players not born within the county, while the chief bowlers were Mallett and A. H. Kardar, who was to become an inspirational captain of Pakistan and for many years, as administrator, the force behind his country's cricket. The Cambridge batting was led by their skipper, Willatt, and by Insole, and Bailey showed distinct merit as an all-rounder. The university won two but lost only two of their fourteen first-class matches.

The varsity match, played at the dull and showery beginning of July, was drawn. Oxford, the clear favourites, assembled the large total of 457, of which Pawson scored 135, Keighley 99 and Donnelly 81. Ousted for a mere 201, Cambridge provided more stalwart resistance in their second innings, with Willatt and Bailey prominent. They were 58 in front with 5 wickets in hand when the game ended. Keighley and Pawson added 226 for the Oxford second wicket, only 17 short of the record for these matches. On the Saturday, 15,000 were present of whom nearly 12,000 paid at the gates, and on the Monday a further 7,000 paid for admission, despite the chilly conditions. They saw several players of an experience uncommon in university circles, one of the ramifications of war, which of course had delayed the education of many.

Another attractive fixture was the Gentlemen and Players match, held a little later in July. Again, 15,000 were present on the opening day, which was a Wednesday, but rain ruined what looked like being an interesting contest. Donnelly's century was matched by Washbrook's, while each received judicious assistance from Edrich and Fletcher respectively. The amateurs recovered from 25 for 5, but were all out for 209 in their second innings. Time and weather counted out a game, which, however outmoded in formula, did provide a valuable setting for English cricketers somewhere between county and Test levels.

Apart from the usual round of public school and services cricket, much of the remaining interest lay in the well-attended festivals with which the summer was concluded. Eddie Paynter, the old Lancashire and England star, had not played first-class cricket since the war, but the perky left-hander dominated the Harrogate festival, with 154 and 73 for the North against the South, and 127 for the Rest against Maurice Leyland's XI. Jackson took 12 for 148 as the North set up a solid victory, while a hundred from Brookes helped the Rest to conquer Leyland's XI.

At Hastings the South of England lost to South Africa and to Sir Pelham Warner's XI, the latter match noteworthy for Compton passing Tom Hayward's 1906 aggregate of 3,518 runs. He was 87 not out in the first innings and, requiring a further 35 runs for the record, he scored, not without some alarums, 86 in the second. Good bowling by Laker assured a victory for Warner's XI. At Kingston-on-Thames the South beat the North in a fine run-feast, in which Fletcher scored 168 and 76 for the losers, and Todd and Holmes were century-makers for the winners. On that same immaculate square, Surrey and Kent defeated Middlesex and Essex in a very similar sort of game, dominated by batting. F. H. Vigar of Essex and Arthur Fagg of Kent made hundreds.

Scarborough was the site of the most well-known festival. The weather held well into September, and holiday-makers basked in the warm sunshine. Only twenty minutes were lost during the three fixtures, the first of which saw Yorkshire lose to MCC. The second game, between the North and South, was, inevitably, a draw. It was, however, an entertaining draw, with fast and furious stroke-play, including centuries from Washbrook, Yardley, Fishlock, Donnelly and Freddie Brown. Then the first-class season was completed with the Players' victory by an innings over the Gentlemen. Howorth, with 8 wickets and 80 runs, was their chief protagonist.

Nothing can or must detract from the achievement of the Middlesex pair, Denis Compton and Bill Edrich. They carved the touchstone against which individual contributions to county cricket have been judged. In his elegant tribute to their activities, R. C. Robertson-Glasgow spoke of the 'communicative' characters of their cricket, the manner in which they conveyed their 'happy philosophy' to spectators and embraced them within the ambit of their performance. It was exactly this delightful *mélange* of enthralling theatre and intimate communion which distinguished the 1947 summer.

It has often been explained how Compton was the more natural player, a mudlark of a genius who transcended quite humble beginnings to combine the magic of a Ranji with the cheek of a Max Miller. The tradition of great professionalism had been to add imperiousness to impeccable technique, after the style of Hobbs or Hammond or Hutton. They combined in abundance, to borrow from *Ruddigore*, 'the manners of a marquis with the morals of a methodist'. The instinctive flair and sheer breezy amusement of Compton was different from this: it was the stuff of folklore, of the self-confident tinker thwarting the lumbering giant, or of Aladdin outwitting Abanazar. If Gilbert and Sullivan might be visited again, Denis Compton was the Pirate King of cricket: 'when I sally forth to seek my prey, I help myself in a royal way'. And, as the Pirate King further explained to the pirates of Penzance, 'I don't think much of our profession, but, contrasted with respectability, it is comparatively honest'.

Bill Edrich was of another school, one that had included adversity on its curriculum, but by 1947 he had overcome these barriers, added judgement and retained unabated vim, and transformed excellence of talent into largesse of riches. A cricketer unremittingly brave and enthusiastic, he was scarcely less than Compton's equal in 1947, by whose side he endeavoured, turning now to *The Gondoliers*, to 'take an attitude not too stately, still sufficiently dignified'.

Such garnerings are the more relevant, for, as Robertson-Glasgow remarked, in comparing Compton and Edrich with G & S, 'in the art of giving pleasure to an English audience, both pairs lack rival'. It is fair to project that analogy, for in many senses the fashion of the enjoyment was similar. Around the cricket grounds of England in 1947, the pleasure that Compton and Edrich proffered was merry, melodious, cleancut and intelligent, yet with some ridiculing of the exalted, cheerily and without malice; all of which were the distinctive traits of the Savoy operas.

It must be apparent, however, from any reading or accurate remembrance of that amiable summer, that they were jostled close by competitors, both in quantities of achievement and qualities of artistry. The figures reveal how bright and masterly were their rivals, even if they tell little of the delicious and handsome taste of it all.

1947 Batting Averages (top ten with 2,000 runs)

	Innings	Runs	Average
D. C. S. Compton	50	3,816	90.85
W. J. Edrich	52	3,539	80.43
C. Washbrook	47	2,662	68.25
L. E. G. Ames	42	2,272	64.91
J. Hardstaff	44	2,396	64.75
L. Hutton	44	2,585	64.62
W. Place	47	2,501	62.52
J. D. Robertson	57	2,760	52.07
L. J. Todd	55	2,312	46.24
A. E. Fagg	56	2,203	43.19

In all, sixteen batsmen scored over 2,000 runs and, with a minimum of eight innings, twenty-nine averaged over 40. There were 364 first-class centuries in 1947, compared with 257 in 1946.

1947 Bowling Averages (top ten with 100 wickets)

	Overs	Wickets	Average
T. W. Goddard	1,451	238	17.30
J. A. Young	1,291	159	17.38
R. Howorth	1,254	164	17.85
G. H. Pope	786	114	18.38
L. B. Muncer	802	107	18.85
C. Gladwin	917	117	19.63
R. Pollard	1,218	144	19.82
C. Cook	1,134	144	20.32
D. V. P. Wright	1,175	177	21.12
E. P. Robinson	1,044	108	21.58

In all, twenty bowlers took 100 wickets and, with a minimum of 10 wickets, eighteen averaged less than 20.

Even these stark figures convey something of the high standards of the year. Given that it has been, perhaps naturally, the habit to emphasise the batting of 1947, it would be compassionate to spare a thought for the oft unsung bowlers. Tom Goddard, so antagonistic a member of a mystery which conventionally reflects patience and stoic endurance, bowled some fifty or sixty overs a game, and took over 200 wickets for the fourth time in his career. That accomplishment, in a summer of glorious batsmanship, is worthy enough to set him alongside Compton and Edrich as what, in modern parlance, might be called 'the men of the season'. It all but brought a Championship title to Gloucestershire. Others – the always fascinating Wright; that stolid all-rounder, Howorth; the hardworking and astute Young; the northern toilers, such as Pollard, Pope and Gladwin – were unabashed by the tidal race of runs that daily washed around them. They stuck to the perspicacious virtues of their craft, and at the season's end they had much to be proud of.

As for the batting, any one of a dozen might have assumed the mantle of maestro had, unhappy thought, neither Compton nor Edrich been in action. Pugnaciously, Cyril Washbrook had commanded respect the year through, while, as if lifted from the cigarette cards of the 1930s, the debonair skills of Les Ames and Joe Hardstaff had likewise been on imperious display. Indeed, and possibly it was an omen too sober for so cheerful and fulfilling a time, almost all the batting, assessed either by abundance or grandeur, was provided by yesteryear's men, for all the top English batsmen were thirty years old or so. Something of the same is true of the bowlers, as Goddard himself exemplified.

There were up-and-coming players. Men like Jim Laker, David Fletcher, Trevor Bailey and, albeit in conscious brevity, Ken Cranston had enjoyed promising seasons, but there was no one, in those two post-years, who arrived and threw down the gauntlet in the way that Compton and Hutton had done as young men in the 1930s. Godfrey Evans was far and away the pick of the early post-war contingent, but, for the rest, there had been few young players to evoke excitement. The relative failure of the English middle-order batting and the reliance on Compton and Edrich as Test bowlers underpins that piece of analysis. Of course, new people had to be tried, but the fact remains that England might have done even better in the Test matches had they recruited Ames, Hardstaff and Goddard.

The sparse statistics of 1947 do constitute a validity of their own. They indicate a buxom substance about the cricket of that summer. Even allowing for the lengthier list of first-class matches (and then, alternatively, tempering that with the stress of such continuous first-class play) it is the weightiness of the performances which are significant. Although we have it dinned into us that the pressures are more intense now, because of the monetary rewards, and thus players proceed with due caution, the facts of 1947 suggest that the top-grade players were prolific without being drearily careful. Both batsmen and bowlers, at the highest level, contrived to interweave in indiscernible and aesthetic pattern the three threads of cricketing design: they were artistic, they were entertaining, they were functional.

They satisfied the traditional and strict canons of this most artistically minded of games; they brought immense joy to the humbler dwellers on the popular sides and, by proxy, to the thousands who followed all these happenings in the newspapers; and they consistently scored lots of runs and took lots of wickets. There was a familiar and welcome predictability about this substantiality. Tom Goddard would regularly and on average take 8 or 9 wickets a match, while Denis Compton would score the equivalent of a century every three or so innings. Frequently, in more modern times, the players who function most successfully are dour, earnest, worthy and boring; and the players who delight do so ephemerally.

Although the mood of 1947 is, perfectly correctly, recalled as one of wondrous occurrences, these events were the consequence of cricketers combining theatrical flair with workaday technique. They managed to find a compound of the lively spirit of the cavalier and the tenacious flesh of the roundhead. No finer example of this ambience is to be found than the existence of so many acknowledged pairs of opening bats. Most counties had a recognised couple, who were household names, as secure and reassuring as a firm of local solicitors; and yet flowing off the tongue as catchily as one of the many comic double-acts which were then the rage on wireless and variety stage. Dodds and Cray; Dyson and Davies; Arnold and

Rogers; Todd and Fagg; Washbrook and Place; Robertson and Brown . . . Even where there was no fully established couple, there was always at least one extremely sound opener, such as John Langridge, Berry, Brookes, Fishlock, Barnett or, of course, Hutton. Indeed, one of the reasons for Yorkshire's fall from grace might have been the lack of a fresh-born Sutcliffe to partner Hutton. Nevertheless, one might wonder aloud whether England in the 1990s might not have preferred possibly eight of those names to some of her current opening hopefuls.

Another illustration might be sought in the variety of bowling, as opposed to the present generation of incessant seamers and hurried, flightless spinners. No self-respecting county XI would have taken the field in 1947 without a left-hand spin bowler. Lancashire with Roberts and Price, and Middlesex with Young and Compton, each had two, while the county teamsheets also produce such names as James Langridge, Sam Cook, Jack Walsh, Vince Broderick, Bertie Buse, Johnny Wardle, Dick Howorth, A.H. Kardar (playing for Warwickshire in the long vacation), Emrys Davies and Horace Hazell. There were certainly plenty of off-spinners about. Apart from Tom Goddard, there were *inter alia* Ray Smith, John Clay, Peter Jackson and Vic Jackson, the young Jim Laker, Robinson of Yorkshire, Jack Mercer, the amateur C. J. Knott, and R. R. Dovey. But perhaps the greatest surprise in terms of modern contrast would lie in the presence of so many leg-spinners. Beginning with the England Test selections of Wright and Hollies, one could continue with such notable performers as the West Indian C. B. Clarke, Roly Jenkins, Jim Sims, Ian Bedford, Peter Smith, Dusty Rhodes and John Ikin.

It was not, therefore, unusual for a county to field, possibly with the decent assistance of all-rounders, five bowlers of varying type: a fastish bowler, a medium-pace bowler, an off-spinner, a leg-spinner and the classic left-hander. Whether or not this blessed relief from the unremitting menu of fast-medium bowling off long runs was the cause, the public actually watched more cricket in the sense of more balls delivered.

Perhaps this can be illustrated by the last great match of the season, to which reference has not yet been made. At the Oval, in the middle of September, the Champion County played the Rest, in a fixture that had lain redundant since 1935. It was a four-day game, and a near Test side was heavily defeated by Middlesex by 9 wickets, only the third time ever the leading county had won this game. Despite his knee being swaddled and strapped, Compton made 246, his highest score on English soil. Edrich scored 180, and the irresistible pair added 210, so that the fixture offered a cameo characteristic of the entire season. Emmett, Yardley and Washbrook tried hard, but a total of 543 was overmuch of a facer and, equally typically, the Middlesex bowlers twice worked their way placidly through the batting. The game needed less than an hour of its fourth day, so that, in just over three days, both sides together delivered 336 overs, something like eighteen an hour. In the context of a four-day game, with a huge buffeting being handed out, with all that means in terms of worrying about and re-setting fields, and remembering that an over replete with struck boundaries and much running takes very much longer than a maiden over – this was a fair rate by any criteria. It certainly meant that there was no deliberate time-wasting when under the lash, of the kind that has led to legislation about over rates.

An even more encouraging example might be culled from Nottingham against Surrey at Trent Bridge when only 18 wickets fell as 1,308 runs were scored, including 706 for 4 by the visitors. On such a pitiless track, it rebounds greatly to the credit of both sides that they laboured away to the tune of 381 overs, that is, an average of just over twenty-one an hour. Spectators received value for money without doubt. A final illustration might be the Middlesex innings of 537 for 2 against Surrey: 118 overs in the day, a most sporting rate of twenty an hour. Nor was it a complete rout, for Middlesex averaged only 4.5 runs an over, not as high as one might have expected from such a score. Surrey maintained strict adherence to the traditional precepts of bowling, and it is unusual that Compton managed only nine 4s in his 137. Edrich had eighteen boundaries in his undefeated 157, as the pair added nearly 300 in a little less than three hours. The tempo of the cricket, as well as the style and design, was ideal.

Nostalgia is an important aspect of the cricket culture. In terms of 1947, it has its role, in part for its direct benignity, in part because the sentient idea of 1947 is as significant as the facts. But that is no reason to shun the less glowing aspects of 1947, or to pretend that all glory has been lost and no progress made. More than most sports, cricket has retained its consistency of grandeur over a lengthy period. Not only have there been great players in every decade, the underlying fundamentals of the game have remained comparatively unchanged, so that comparison is more legitimate than in other games. Although there has been much superficial tinkering with the rules and the conditions of play, the basic formula completed by the late Victorians has been so revered that no attempt has been made to alter that foundation. Moreover, the relatively long life of the cricketer has also made for pleasing overlaps of champions, old and new, playing alongside one another. A chain, for instance, of Grace, Hayward, Hobbs, Hammond, Bradman, Hutton and Compton, Harvey, May, Cowdrey . . . and onward to the major West Indian batsmen of the last decades, is both a pleasurable and a genuine one to link together.

Thus there is no way that a great player of the 1980s or 1990s need feel discomfited by comparison with Compton and Edrich. A Hick, a Gavaskar, a Viv Richards, a Border, an Imran Khan, a Richard Hadlee – just to take a casual trawl around the cricketing nations – will stand muster any time and any place. And there *were* weaknesses in 1947. Although there were superb specialist fieldsmen among its cricketers, the general tone and energy of fielding – and probably of running between the wickets – has improved since those times. The pre-war veteran, the untrained youth, the occasional amateur, the gentlemanly skipper, the disdainful bowler: they all meant that practically every team had a couple of passengers or, at least, one or two who could not now be afforded in the quick passion of one-day cricket. Of course, there have been few to equal Washbrook as a cover-point, or his colleague, John Ikin, as a close catcher, whilst Godfrey Evans was outstanding as a wicket-keeper. Such individual instances could be duplicated over and over from the ranks of 1947, but the fact remains that almost every county side today is a well-drilled and co-ordinated fielding machine.

But that was not the widest or the most significant gap between 1947 and an English season today. Not least because of contracted overseas players or the visiting tourists, one would now be likely to witness bowling of high pace during an English summer. There was no bowler of true speed playing in 1947. Neither England nor the South Africans could find one; perhaps prophetically, Pritchard, the New Zealander playing with Warwickshire, was regarded, when on occasional song, as being the speediest. There were several to cast in the part of shrewd and honest journeymen, plenty of seasoned, nagging, unremitting deliverers of fast-medium bowling; but there was no Larwood nor Trueman nor Michael Holding on show. This must eventually mean that 1947 lacked an attribute of perfection, for, as John Arlott reminded in his elegant essay on 1947, the violent beauty of sheer pace, its coiling of menace within loveliness, is an essence of cricket.

The more pragmatic observer might have snorted at the aesthetic view, and pointed up the practical lesson. Next year we would enjoy the undiluted essence – Lindwall and Miller would be discharging considerable menace and loveliness around our cricket grounds – and our batsmen had gone another full summer without any realistic preparation for such a contest.

Few would cavil, despite this one insufficiency, that 1947 was one of the best; for many, *the* best of seasons. Denis Compton remains the presiding genius of the year, for its style, spirit and pace were the ones he so gleefully personified. The legends are as uncountable as those of Ulysses, and they suggest that the two men of action were not unlike in character. Denis Compton was the man who arrived late in the dressing-room after a jolly binge; the man who forgot his kit and was constantly borrowing gear from protesting team-mates; the man who, rushing out to Tom Goddard, fell with his feet locked, and yet still managed to sweep a 4; the man who, although quick enough between the wickets, might have been nicknamed the Frankie Howerd of callers; the man who was so completely disorganised that the accountant, Bagenal Harvey, requested in 1949 to bring order to his benefit and other affairs, built out of that motley disarray the first English agency for sportsmen.

So the stories roll off the presses and off the tongues. The imagery, of course, was not Grecian: it was much closer in time and locale. Compton, ex-soldier though he was, played his cricket as the public recognised a wartime fighter pilot might have played it. It was to do with 'the Few' of recent memory; the eccentric garb and the racy slang, and that strange mix of swank and modesty of the flying men. It was to do with Spitfires and Biggles; and, at the comic end, it was to do with Jimmy Edwards and his handlebar moustache, or radio's *Much Binding in the Marsh*, with Richard Murdoch and Kenneth Horne exchanging air station fatuities. He evoked the great, early war days. Keith Miller was to cast the same spell, and for similar reasons.

Denis Compton, then, eschewed the bureaucratic route and yearned for the venturesome road. The side of the story not often told is the one not often told about the wartime RAF. What he did was to weave, often laboriously, from one cricket ground to another and score near enough 4,000 runs, including eighteen centuries. He did so against frequently, if not invariably, keen and high-class bowling, and he sustained his form through hot weather and cold, in all kinds of conditions, and even, at the latter end of the season, with his infamous knee a sore problem. It really is time we heard a little bit more of the less colourful portion of the fable: the rigorous underlay of technique; the fierce commitment, to himself, to his teams, to his public; the dedication of mental stamina and concentration; the steadying fire of rightful ambition, in the sense of a relentless determination to reveal and never waste his remarkable talent.

That colossal endeavour should be a significant part of the record, especially in an age where the winsome bat sometimes attracts the subsidiary adjective of 'willowy' or 'casual'. Denis Compton was rarely, for all his ebullient informality, lbw playing across the line, bowled with uplifted bat, or caught from a lazy swish – like, as the northern mothers of 1947 might have said, 'some we could mention'.

Reference has been made to the sometimes unholy communion established between Compton and those who watched or heard and read of his daring exploits. In *Beyond a Boundary*, C. L. R. James wrote with insight about the relation of W. G. Grace to his adoring fans: 'The point is that whatever his fatigue, he could take no notice of it. The crowds and the people made of every innings a Test innings. . . If Grace could be so often and so long at his best it was because so much depended on it, so many hundreds and thousands of people, high and low, were expecting him to be at his best, even to exceed it, as he had so often done in the past'. As C.L.R. James goes on to remind, we understand very little of 'the nourishment given to the hero by the crowd', of how the slumped actor or the sagging politician will suddenly recover complete command in response to the faithful audience.

This dimension must surely have been part of the cavalcade of 1947. The crowds must have willed the players to vaster effort, and the players must have been lifted by that collective vibration of yearning. The star players, the Comptons and Hardstaffs and Huttons, were, of course, the chief givers and receivers in this marriage of cumulative glory, but many other players and whole teams were also party to this communal transaction.

If great players and great crowds are inseparable partners in the creation of great cricket, then 1947 was the most eloquent portrait of the phenomenon. It was announced that some three millions were in attendance at the first-class fixtures of 1947, of whom it has been computed that 2,300,900 paid at the turnstiles. This suggests an amazing average of over 10,000 spectators every day at every game, something not now common at several self-respecting Football League clubs. Crowds of 30,000 were not uncommon. Yorkshire, who suffered in the cricketing sense, benefited at the gate, with nearly 300,000 people turning up at their four main grounds. Kent housed nearly 200,000, half as much again as in 1946, and twice as many as in 1939. Some 50,000 went through the juvenile turnstiles, an encouraging sign. These were county records for both Yorkshire and Kent, while Kent's membership rose to over 3,300. The membership at Essex topped 3,000 for the first time, whilst Lancashire's increased to 5,000. Benefits were automatically excellent. The £4,000 for James Langridge was a Sussex record, and Bill Bowes's £8,000 doubled the previous Yorkshire best. Frank Lee of Somerset and Todd of Kent also did extremely well.

In 1960 the paying custom had dropped to a million, half the 1947 figure. In 1981 it was less than 200,000, something like Kent's own total for 1947. That represented an average of around 300 a day at all matches, although, of course, members would have added a few to these solitary and scattered figures. Today, and discounting one-day games, a county counts itself lucky to attract 10,000 paying spectators to its dozen or so three-day games. In 1947 the first day of the University match brought in 11,748 paying spectators.

There in a nutshell lies the bountiful success of 1947 and the degree of failure since. In the last analysis, the amorphous crowd, that packet of assembled statistics, was to be the most important component in the story of 1947. It appeared to prove beyond a peradventure that the conservatives had been right. It demonstrated that the good old British public wanted nothing more nor less than good old British cricket, and that the case of the reconstructionists was shallow and ill-based. Arguments for reform and change were effortlessly stilled by the clink of cash at the turnstiles and the broadening smiles of the county treasurers.

The conclusion drawn was wholly understandable, and it would be churlish to fault those who made statements beginning, 'There can't be much wrong with a game which can attract three million people . . .' Nonetheless, it was entirely the wrong conclusion, as events were shortly to prove.

PART THREE

Coda

7

The Years of Reality

The first hint of anti-climax occurred almost immediately. A little reluctantly, MCC had agreed to tour the West Indies. After the tiring trip to Australia and New Zealand and the bustle of the 1947 summer, this reluctance was understandable, especially as England would have to face the Australians in the following summer (the Australians actually arrived in England before the party returned from the West Indies), and then there was a scheduled visit to South Africa to bear in mind for the winter of 1948-49. It was, for the blood of conservative authorities, too frenetic. It was a cataract of tours and visits which while common, if still criticised, now, was regarded as insufficiently leisurely, and certainly more stressful than in pre-war years. However, everyone was anxious to restore normality, and after the long lay-off all the Test-playing countries were naturally keen to resume rivalries.

The West Indies were the least regarded of the cricketing nations, with the possible exception of New Zealand. In three tours of England, they had failed to win a Test, although on their own grounds and usually against less than full strength sides, they had fared better. Of eight Tests played on the two previous MCC tours, they had won three to England's two, with three drawn. With a great batsman like George Headley (who, despite the ravages of time, captained his side in the first Test) and an all-rounder of the class of Learie Constantine, the West Indies had never been a pushover, but they had appeared to lack both talent in depth and a modicum of professional grit.

Had the cricketing experts more carefully studied the reports of wartime and post-war cricket in the West Indies, there might have been less surprise at the improved standards of batting. Surely, for example, attention had been drawn to the events of February 1946 in Port of Spain, when Clyde Walcott (314 not out) and Frank Worrell (255 not out) added 574 for the Barbados fourth wicket against Trinidad: and the game was saved with a double century from G. E. Gomez and an accompanying hundred from Ken Trestrail. Gomez had been a young member of the 1939 party to visit England; now he, Headley and Stollmeyer from that tour were joined by Worrell, Weekes, Walcott, Carew, Ganteaume and Christiani. Most of these were to make merry at some stage against the Englishmen, and, although the bowling was not of this quality, it was stronger and better-motivated than previous West Indian teams.

MCC sent no more than a second string. Thirteen players who were to play against the Australians in 1948 either would not or could not tour. Compton, Edrich, Washbrook, Barnett, Bedser, Wright, Hollies, Yardley, Crapp, Dollery, Emmett and Young remained in England, while Hutton only joined the party when it was threatened with utter collapse. G. O. Allen captained, although he had seen little first-class play of late, and injured himself skipping on the voyage. In his mid-40s, he was a man of ripe experience, and the notion was presumably that he should bring-on his hopefuls, lest they be needed to support the senior players over the next two or three years.

His assistant-manager and reserve wicket-keeper was Billy Griffith, who made 140 – his first ever first-class century – opening the batting in his first ever Test match. And he did not even open for his county! It was an admirable feat, but the causes for his needing to attempt it were depressing. Allen had found himself, by the time of this the second Test, surrounded by illness and injury. Every newspaper seemed to bring fresh and alarming data of malaria, chipped bones, strained muscles, carbuncles and other ailments. From the time the ship had set forth on its long and laboured passage, the visit and the circumstances surrounding it had proved to be ill-fated. The tropical heat told, and there had perhaps been inadequate acclimatisation, especially for men recently reared on British rations.

It was not an untalented group. Ken Cranston, the vice-captain, determined to squeeze every last drop from his planned two years of top-class cricket, played usefully, and Jim Laker found matters to his liking. Evans continued to polish his reputation, while Hardstaff, Robertson, Brookes and the Lancashire opener, Winston Place, gave quality to the early batting, at least when all of them could be mustered. Naturally, the arrival of Hutton bolstered this side of things, and Robertson and Place both scored Test hundreds. The bowling was less challenging, for Allen himself could not sustain his speed for very long, and Harold Butler was a malaria sufferer. Of the younger players, little was heard of Tremlett, Wardle and Smithson, although they all won caps. Only Johnny Wardle of that trio was to gain further honours.

The first two Tests were drawn, Robertson being the saviour in the second of those games. In rain-affected conditions at Georgetown England lost, following on, after an excellent maiden Test century from Worrell. At Kingston, where Weekes in turn obliged with a first Test hundred, the West Indies won by 10 wickets, and took the series comfortably. It was the first time England had toured the West Indies and not won a Test match. So strong had been the West Indian batting that Carew and Ganteaume both scored centuries but could not retain their places.

It was, then, a somewhat battered, bewildered and perhaps even ashamed party which slunk back to English shores, for, while allowing for the ill-luck, they had been bravely out-played. It was the first tiny dent in the glowing self-confidence that the successes of 1947 had created.

At least the West Indian failure had taken place in a far-distant land against a mixture of mainly older players who had not quite made the grade and younger players who had been offered a chance to do so. In 1948, with the fanfares blaring to herald the Australians, there was nowhere to hide. Any remnant of hope that England had survived the war unscathed, and were in a position to combat an international team of undoubted quality and confidence, was soon to vanish.

The crowds remained buoyant as cricket once more proved itself to be a popular spectator sport. There were record audiences for the all-conquering Australians. Over 130,000 watched the Manchester Test, and a record 160,000 saw the Leeds game. County treasurers were delighted as, day after day, grounds were packed and coffers filled; and the Australians must also have been pleased, for they took home a profit approaching £80,000, twice as much as they had ever done before.

The cricket was, however, one-sided, especially after the balanced matches of 1947 which, pleasantly enough for the patriotic fan, had tilted towards England. Test matches apart, the Australians annihilated the county opposition. They were unbeaten in their thirty-one first-class games, and often won by great margins; half their victories were by an innings, and, against Essex, they scored 721 in a day – although, at least, Essex did dismiss all of them. E. W. Swanton calculated that eleven Australians scored forty-seven centuries, while five opponents made seven against them; and that, whereas they failed to reach 200 only twice, their opponents were out for less than 200 no less than thirty-seven times.

Watching England in the Tests was rather like Christians being asked to sit and watch the lions perform at the Coliseum in ancient Rome. All one could do was pray for a small miracle which might temporarily limit or restrict the proud and arrogant victors.

England began with two near-routs. Faced by Lindwall and Miller working up a pace which had not been witnessed in this country since the heady days of Larwood, England collapsed disastrously. Only Bedser and Laker salvaged any self-respect on a Trent Bridge wicket which was easy enough of itself, but where the climate favoured swing. With Wright ailing, Bradman and Hassett gradually mastered some rather ordinary and defensive bowling, and 509 runs were assembled. In difficult circumstances, both as to the state of the game and the weather, Compton now played one of his most illustrious innings, and it was his 184 which made it necessary for Australia to bat a second time. They ran out winners by 8 wickets.

At Lord's, and although strains periodically thwarted both Lindwall and Miller, England were even more outplayed. The Australians accumulated massive scores, and, for their part, the English proffered puny ones. The eventual margin was an astonishing 409 runs. Hutton, showing less affection for extreme pace since his forearm had been weakened and shortened by injury during the war, was dropped for the following Test. The nation was aghast. It was apparently a ruse to encourage both Hutton and his colleagues, but it was viewed as an extraordinary decision. Len Hutton had played well enough in the first Test (an untroubled 74 in the second innings), and as he was judged, alongside Compton, as the inheritor of the mantle of Hobbs and Hammond, the public wondered anxiously about the crisis. It was as if Montgomery had been called home from the desert at the height of the El Alamein campaign.

Whatever the effect on Hutton, the effect on his replacements was negligible. The two batsmen brought into the side around this period – George Emmett and Jack Crapp of Gloucestershire – did little or nothing, and the former won only one cap. It was once again Compton who rallied the regiment and added to heroic legend in the third Test at Old Trafford. With England reeling, he sallied forth, his forehead stitched and plastered following a sickening blow from Lindwall. With stalwart help from the non-commissioned officers of the tail, Compton, like the young subaltern in the old school stories, drove and smote the enemy for 145 runs.

Pollard had dislodged Sidney Barnes from his customary and talkative post at short mid-on with a sharp drive into the kidneys. With 363 on the board and the Australian batting already disrupted, Bedser and Pollard bowled well, and England suddenly found themselves with a long second innings lead. In the face of some dangerously short-pitched bowling, Washbrook and Edrich (both of whom must have been expecting the 'Hutton treatment') helped place England in a very strong position. But, then, with a lead of over 300 and with 7 wickets in hand, the rains visited, and a day and a half was lost.

Naturally disappointed, the English party moved on to Leeds for the fourth Test, and Hutton was recalled to open with Washbrook. As if mightily stung by his humiliation, Hutton proceeded to play defiantly against pace, not only in 1948, but thereafter, and one of the features of the excellent Leeds match was the two opening stands by England of over 100 each. With the young Neil Harvey and Sam Loxton in belligerent form, the English were outpaced, their opponents matching the Englishmen's 496 with 458, but in half the time. It was an omen of sorts. Declaring after a couple of overs on the fifth day, Yardley set the Australians 404 to win – which they comfortably did. It was the first time either side had won following a declaration against it. It is difficult at this distance to assess the pros and cons of that historic day. It was a 7-wicket victory, with Morris and Bradman scoring large centuries after early alarms. But they were abetted by a disgraceful England performance, in which the attack lacked shape and the fielding was mediocre. Crucial chances went a-begging, and even Godfrey Evans was by no means blameless. It was one of those cricketing days which contrived to touch both zenith and nadir.

This had been an excellent game, but England were properly chastened. Changes, enforced and deliberate, were made for the final Test at the Oval, but they were to be of no avail. Although, after interminable rain, the pitch was sluggish, Lindwall ran through the English batting, and they could manage no more than a beggarly 52. Of these, Hutton played an innings some praised as one of his most able, scored 30 and was last out. Although, in a famed moment, Hollies bowled Bradman for a duck, the Australians batted with relish, and England, collapsing for less than 200, lost by an innings. The series was thus lost by four games to love, with one draw: it was quite humiliating.

What explanations could be made should be offered. Some felt that this Australian XI was the finest team ever assembled, and that there was no disgrace in defeat. The openers were Barnes and Morris, obdurately playing off the back foot in trenchant and profitable manner. The shrewd experience of Hassett and the youthful flair of Harvey benefited from this stable platform, and above all there was the tireless Bradman, now in his 40th year, but busily gathering nearly 2,500 runs at an average of 89. Keith Miller was the leading all-rounder of his epoch, whilst Lindwall, believed by many judges to be the pick of fast bowlers throughout history, was himself a valued batsman. Australia were fortunate in that their menacing fast attack was also capable of scoring lots of runs. W. A. Johnston, a left-handed quick bowler, provided the perfect support for the Lindwall/Miller duo, and Tallon was a splendid wicket-keeper-batsman. Sam Loxton and Bill Brown were other useful performers. Ian Johnson, the off-spinner, and Ernie Toshack, the left-hander, were the chief spin bowlers, although they were utilised mainly to offer respite to the fast bowlers. If one were to compare this Australian team with, for instance, their predecessors of the early 1920s, or the great England XI at the turn of the century, or one or other of the versatile West Indian sides of more recent times, then one might have to pause over the spin bowling. Judged by the strictest of classical criteria, the 1948 Australians lacked a spin bowler of world class, a man such as O'Reilly, Grimmett or Mailey. That apart, they were well-nigh faultless.

Although England were on the receiving end of some fearful drubbings, the record indicates that, over the first two post-war series against Australia, it was weakness in attack rather then defence which led to these humiliations. It is true that they were dismissed for less than 200 in as many as seven out of the twenty innings they played; but they did score over 300 in another nine of those innings, and, given decent bowling, that has often been enough to save a match. And this was against a very superior batch of quick bowlers. Compton, Hutton and Washbrook each made successful contributions. On the other hand, the Australians never collapsed once in the first ten post-war Tests, and their 221 at Old Trafford was easily the lowest of their fifteen substantive innings. On eleven of these occasions they topped 300, including four times when they passed the 500 mark.

The bowling was often feeble and over-reliant on the indomitable Bedser, and this probably stemmed from the maturity of the team. It averaged about 32 years, whereas the team that had played Australia in 1938 had averaged 28. That side included two or three over-thirties, while the teams of 1946-47 and 1948 had as many as nine on occasion. Although this meant the batsmen were very experienced, it left the bowlers too long in the tooth. The deprivations of war were beginning to tell: it is a telling fact that no leading English opening bowler, with the exception of Trevor Bailey, was born between 1919 and 1929; that is, who might have been of an age to serve an apprenticeship to the bowling craft during the sterile war years. In particular, the one lament of the 1947 season was underscored by the Australian visit: there had been no bowling at high pace in 1947, and English cricket had none to offer in 1948.

The swings of the pendulum are curious. Between the wars, at least after McDonald and Gregory had completed their depredations of the English batting, the Australians had relied almost totally on a stream of high-class spin bowlers – during a spell when England had been able to turn to Larwood, Voce, Allen, Bowes, and

Farnes. In the post-war years, England had only pop-guns to trade with the Australian cannon, and it was not surprising that, in the aftermath of the bodyline controversy, Australia frequently bowled an alarming ration of short-pitched deliveries. Indeed, even in 1948 they were booed for so doing at Trent Bridge, the erstwhile home of Larwood and Voce, although at Old Trafford, after Compton's frightening injury, Bradman did sympathetically resort to slow bowling. Of course, it was Bradman who made the wholesale difference between what otherwise would have been fairly even batting, and it is no discredit to Yardley to report the obvious, that Bradman was his superior in tactical know-how. Australia fielded superbly well, and only at wicket-keeping could England claim some supremacy – and even in this department Tallon was immensely skilled.

There was some relief during the MCC tour of South Africa over the following winter of 1948–49, for F. G. Mann, shrugging off his inexperience, exhorted his troops sufficiently to win two Tests, albeit by excitingly slender margins, with the other three matches drawn. It was an enjoyable and sporting series, an amicable mirror of 1947. These years of such friendly relations were to be a strong factor when cricketers had to face the unwelcome, but cruel and monstrous, truth about South African social and political values; it was that much harder to associate such inhumane mores with past comradeship.

Such ethical musings are incidental to the main thread of the tale, for in truth the cricket was more interesting than classic. The South Africans, rather as in 1947 on English soil, appeared to lack a little in confidence and presence, and they were slow and reluctant to challenge. For their part, the Englishmen provided the mix as before. It was the old faithfuls who scored the runs, with Compton and Hutton, in their contrasting styles, showing excellent form. Washbrook, too, was in good heart, and, at Johannesburg, Hutton and he assembled 359 for the first wicket, still an English record against all countries. With assistance from the likes of Crapp, Watkins of Glamorgan and Mann (who had succeeded to the Middlesex captaincy in 1948), enough runs were put together for a middling attack to control an indifferent opposition. Bedser, Gladwin and Jenkins were the key bowlers. England won the first and last Tests: the former at Durban where, in a frantic and nerve-wracking finish, it needed a leg-bye off the last ball; and the latter at Port Elizabeth, where England bravely made 174 in an hour and a half on the final day.

In 1949 it was the turn of lowly New Zealand to tour England, and, from one viewpoint, the authenticity of English cricket was quietly laid bare by this trip. They were led by Walter Hadlee, and included, unprecedentedly, two world-class bats in the stylish left-handers Bert Sutcliffe and Martin Donnelly, together with the up-and-coming talent of young John Reid. The bowling was not quite so impressive, but it was steady, and New Zealand lost only one game on that tour. There were four Tests, and they were each drawn. It was probably a conscious – and successful – strategy on the part of the visitors to demonstrate that the three-day Tests to which they were relegated were somewhat insulting to so well-balanced a team, and it was soon clear that there was no way the impoverished English bowling was going to make the essential inroads. Equally, the English batting was able to control matters when New Zealand were the field, and although there was some attractive batting for the spectators, who turned out in goodly numbers, it was a cricketing cul de sac. The imbalance of the England side was made painfully apparent during that pleasant summer of 1949.

The winter of 1949–50 was a blank one for England, something that would be unheard of today. Then in 1950 the West Indies paid their first visit since the traumatic summer of 1939, when rumours and counter-rumours of war had marred the cricket, as so much else of normal life. The West Indians were offered four Tests – hitherto they had been granted only three – and, in part because of the stalemate of 1949, the period of play was extended to five days. It was acknowledged that the West Indian batting was of the highest order, but their bowling was something of an unknown quantity, and the tour began uneasily for the visitors. The first Test at Old Trafford led to a heavy defeat for them. Godfrey Evans had scored his maiden first-class century in impish mood, and then, on a pitch breaking apart like the crumbling of a stale crust, Eric Hollies and Bob Berry, the Lancashire left-hand spin bowler, routed them.

Already, however, the partnership of Alf Valentine and Sonny Ramadhin had been showing dividends in the county matches, and many realised that the Manchester game had been abnormal. Stories circulated about the primitive innocence from which these two skilful bowlers sprang: it was said that they knew nothing of cricket lore or social etiquette, so abruptly had they been dragged from the poor circumstances where their latent prowess had been fortuitously spotted. At Lord's, with sweet aptness, they combined with the brilliant array of their batting colleagues to secure a victory by 326 runs. The left-handed Valentine had match figures of 7 for 127, in over one hundred overs, and, as counterpoint to his severe orthodoxy, the fizzing, variable spin of Ramadhin brought him 11 for 152.

It was a famous victory, and it was also a spectacular and patently convincing one, feted cheerfully by the West Indian contingent, representative, of course, of a rapidly swelling band. Calypso and dance were featured among the sedate appurtenances of Lord's.

Nor was this some freak result. The West Indies proceeded to win the final two Tests. Worrell and Weekes scored mightily at Trent Bridge to set up a 10-wicket win, and another huge total at the Oval established the base for an innings victory. It was the colourful era of the three Ws; Frank Worrell, Everton Weekes and, less prominently on this tour, Clyde Walcott. The sturdy planks laid by the opening batsmen, Stollmeyer and Rae, should be recalled, whilst Gomez was also among the runs. In point of fact, eight of the tourists made 1,000 runs; and yet, ultimately, it was 'those two little friends of mine' who unlocked the doors on these well-merited victories. Ramadhin had 133 wickets and Valentine 123 during the summer, and this included a joint bag of 59 in the four Tests.

It seemed that the English batsmen could no longer play either top-class pace or spin. Hutton had one masterly innings, and Washbrook grafted away over a couple of centuries; otherwise, and apart from occasional glimpses of form from Reg Simpson or Gilbert Parkhouse, all was dross. The bowling had, after the first Test, been butchered. It had been put to the sword perhaps more comprehensively than the Australians had done, with great totals conjured up at breathtaking pace.

Everyone heaped praise on the West Indians, as well they might, and although there may well have been some valiant smiles through the stifled tears, there was a general and authentic regard for the

West Indians. It was recognised that they had come to maturity as a cricketing nation, and that, importantly, they had arrived with panache.

That said, it was England's lowest ebb. Australia had won Test matches in England, of course – but, apart from a single win for South Africa in 1935, no one else had. One must also bear in mind the view of the colonies extant in the immediate post-war period. It was before there was recognition of the deep nature of racism, and the British public probably believed, in a hazy and unformulated way, that somehow the white Anglo-Saxon was a superior fellow. John Goddard's captaincy – typically, he was the well-to-do son of white settlers – underlined the point. The West Indies, like England, had Gentlemen and Players, with the additional dimension that there was an ethnic categorisation as well.

Thus there can be no doubt that the calamitous loss at Lord's, together with the two further defeats, was observed with something like horror and foreboding by both the cricketing Establishment and the general public. In the world of cricket, it had the same stunning effect as was to occur in 1953 when Hungary came to Wembley and disconcerted the England football team.

What might, then, be called 'cricket's Hungary' occurred just three years after the roseate glow of 1947, just as England's football débâcle at the hands of the Hungarians came only a few years after Great Britain's 6–1 defeat of the Rest of Europe. This was also in 1947, and it was described by Brian Glanville in a phrase which could have been deployed for the 1947 cricket season: 'a brilliant sunset'. Football was subject to other melancholy events, like the 1–0 defeat of England by USA, a scratch side captained by a Wrexham reject, in the first World Cup for which the English had entered. This was also in 1950, and the disgrace was witnessed by astonished Brazilians at Belo Horizonte.

The analogies with other sports were thick on the ground, and often for the same reasons. Britain, the fount of modern sport, was smugly complacent about its supremacy, little noting either the debilitating effects of the war on sport in the United Kingdom or, possibly of greater significance, the way in which other nations had advanced in the sporting sense. The 1948 Olympiad was a grave disappointment for the British, for there was nothing to savour. The

United States grabbed a hatful of gold medals, while the heroine of the games was Fanny Blankers-Koen, the Dutch housewife who won four gold medals. In boxing, Bruce Woodcock was the British White Hope of the era, but alas, his career was a mixture of misfortune and ineffectiveness and by 1950 it was dashed forever.

Cricket's national disasters were, therefore, of a part with the overall decline in sporting prestige after the war, or, at least, after the false dawn of anticipation evoked by events in the immediate post-war years. As with other aspects of national life, peace brought its brief honeymoon of hope, followed by a less sweet and less shallow phase of aching reality.

Of course, the summer of 1947 had not been exclusively a matter of international cricket: the Tests had been marvellously played against the canvas of a most exciting county competition. As the national team now lost its way a little, so did the county game grow less vivid and attractive, certainly measured against the delights of 1947.

The 1948 title was unexpectedly taken by Glamorgan, whose previous best performances had been in 1946 when they were sixth. Aside from Warwickshire in 1911 and Derbyshire in 1936, it was the first time the title had gone outside the senior six or seven counties, and as such it was a major surprise. Perhaps churlishly, commentators pointed to the distraction of the Australian tour, which kept Test players out of a number of county games. Nonetheless, Glamorgan won thirteen games under the combative leadership of Wilfred Wooller, and edged four points clear of Surrey. Their veteran bowler, J. C. Clay, had a hand in the crucial match against Hampshire at Bournemouth, fittingly taking 9 for 79, as Glamorgan made sure of the Championship. This was a wetter summer, and a key to their success was the spin bowling of Muncer, late of Middlesex, who took 139 wickets at an average of roughly 16. With enthusiastic fielding, and with expert support from Hever, another ex-Middlesex player, Watkins, Parkhouse, W. E. Jones, and Emrys Davies, Glamorgan forced their way to the top. One cannot but cheer, for the sight of the underdog romping to the lead is always exhilarating. Nonetheless, there must also be an expressed note of concern, for this was no more than a workmanlike outfit, whose success was bound to cast doubts on the general standards of the tournament.

F. G. Mann's Middlesex, who had been a close third in 1948, mounted a strong campaign in 1949, especially in the latter half of the season, when they won their last five games. Yorkshire, recuperating steadily after their unsatisfactory display of 1947, were showing signs of a new-found determination, and, like Middlesex, they won fourteen games. The season ended in an interesting struggle between them, with both sides level on 192 points, the first shared Championship since 1889. (Curiously it was again shared in 1950, this time by Lancashire and Surrey.) Lancashire had been one of the most consistent of post-war counties, and now, assisted by remarkable close catching, the off-spinner, Roy Tattersall, took 163 wickets, often on helpful wickets, and they looked likely champions. Surrey, much recovered from their low placement of 1946, were on the verge of their decade of triumph. They won eight of their last nine games to overtake Lancashire.

There were similarities about several of these victories. Compared with the heady days of 1947, with cavalier batsmanship carrying the gaudy banner, it was the methodical testing primarily of off-spin – Muncer at Glamorgan; Tattersall at Lancashire; Appleyard at Yorkshire – which earned these lower-key Championship titles. In 1951 Eric Hollies had 145 victims with the low trajectory of his brisk leg-spin, and Warwickshire won the title. It was another blow in favour of the less fashionable counties, but the manner of the victory – which was by a large margin – was about efficiency, rather than entertainment. A small group of dour and well-motivated professionals, led by Tom Dollery, doyen of this generation of modern 'pro' captains, laboriously scaled the mountain. None was needed for international or representative matches, and, to the acid chagrin of some critics, only two of them were born in Warwickshire.

Surrey's lengthy epoch of constant success in the Championship during the 1950s was almost entirely the consequence of excellent bowling. The fielding was keen, but, apart from the cool nobility of Peter May, the batting was ordinary. The attack was well-nigh world class. It consisted of Alec Bedser, (only Maurice Tate, George Hirst or George Lohmann would challenge him for the stock bowling niche in an All-England XI); Jim Laker, perhaps the finest off-spinner of all time: Tony Lock, probably England's best left-hand spinner in the post-war era; and Peter Loader, a quick bowler unlucky to find himself bracketed with Statham and Trueman in terms of his career. Often provided with friendly pitches, they imposed an effortless control on the county competition, and Surridge and then Peter May led them to seven consecutive titles.

Surrey were positive enough, but ill-balanced. Although many, not least Surrey supporters, were content with such attacking fervour, there were, equally, those who yearned for handsome batting, at least in some degree of parity. Some argued that Surrey attendances actually decreased as the decade wore on, simply because the games were a trifle one-sided and, lacking the sparkle of high-class batting, dull. That may have been a simplistic interpretation. We have already noted the alarming drop in cricket attendances since about 1950, and Surrey may well have been suffering along with everyone else. Because of the entanglement of social causes and sporting faults endemic from 1950 in British society, it is difficult to assess the comparative effects of poorer cricket and socio-cultural changes – an endeavour to unravel that conundrum will be the basis of the next chapter.

What must be accepted is that the cricket did worsen in quality. The purest measure of this has been provided by Rowland Bowen in his *Cricket: a history of its growth and development throughout the world*. Published in 1970, and thus neatly judging the phase of English first-class cricket prior to the full and detailed predominance of one-day cricket, sponsorship and overseas recruitment, it is, as might be predicted of Rowland Bowen, a dark and pessimistic account. It is right to add that cricket has not deteriorated as fatally as he then anticipated, but his statistical formulation was sombre enough.

He pointed out that no batsman since 1949 had, apart from in 1959 and 1961, made 3,000 runs in a season, and yet it had been accomplished sixteen times in the score or so of seasons between the wars. The assemblage of 2,000 runs in a season had also, he argued, decreased, so that, for instance, only three batsmen reached that target in the period 1963–68; while the best aggregate for 1967 was only 2,089, the worst since 1898. There had, he continued, been only four individual innings of 300 between 1951 and 1969, and the average number of centuries a year was sixty lower in 1956–68 than 1919–35. Only 149 hundreds were struck in 1965, the lowest since 1910. The seasons 1968 and 1969 were the first since 1891 in which there had been no team total of 500, and the 1969 highest was, so to say, the lowest since 1878.

Lest anyone thought this was all down to improved bowling, Rowland Bowen reminded that no bowler had taken 200 wickets in a season since 1957, and only four had managed this since the war, compared to the summers 1922–39 when only twice had this not been achieved. In 1969, the last year of his analysis, only five bowlers took 100 wickets, the worst since 1889, and the top aggregate – 109 victims – was the lowest for the leading wicket taker, in a complete season, for a hundred years. From 1895 to 1939, an average of five or six players per season had managed the double; since the war this had dropped to under three, including four seasons with no double and six with only one. Bowen concluded his sobering testimony with figures about the slump in scoring rates and, had he gloomily wished to voice even more discouragement, he might have said much the same for over rates.

This may provide morbid endorsement for those who grumble, usually without much evidence, about the decline of sporting heroics. Few would, in fact, deny that quality has declined in something like the fashion Bowen calculated. Certainly, for a variety of reasons, the cricket Establishment finally moved to a wholesale series of reforms thereafter, although, again, these were the result of that same mixed compound of economic problems and cricketing solecisms.

On the credit side, it might be pressed that there was a major levelling, either up or down, of the counties, as the success of Glamorgan and Warwickshire testified, and that this involved some spread of ability; there were, for instance, no timorous counties to be bowled out cheaply or against whom runs might be scored with abandon. Nevertheless, quality did appear to deteriorate.

Internationally, as the West Indians of 1950 demonstrated, there was a similar leavening, so that soon there were no junior Test countries, none who, home or away, might not give their one-time seniors a close-run game. Such changes may cloud the vision and delude watchers into a belief that it was simply the collapse of, in this case, English cricket.

England was to produce some worthy sides and some masterly cricketers in the decade of the 1950s and beyond. Peter May and Colin Cowdrey, perhaps David Sheppard and Ted Dexter, inherited the mantle of Hammond and Compton with some aplomb, while Fred Trueman and Brian Statham – and, all too briefly, Frank Tyson – might challenge even Harold Larwood, when men and women sit around winter fires and select England's best-ever side. Jim Laker would assuredly be an automatic choice for such an ethereal XI, although no other post-war spinner would attract consideration. The wicket-keeping sustained its efficacy, from Evans to Alan Knott, John Murray and Bob Taylor, and, along with an overall improvement in fielding, that remains a proud tradition. What must, however, be added is that, since this generation, and thinking of the last twenty years, there have been precious few England cricketers whom one would justly discuss in the same breath as Hobbs and Hammond and Hutton. Only two spring readily to mind; two cricketers of vividly contrasting styles and, it must be added, as colourfully contrasting flaws: one refers, of course, to the impeccable defensive technology of Geoffrey Boycott, and the titanic belligerence of Ian Botham.

Whatever the compensations, it must be admitted that the bubble burst. The unmitigated joy of 1947, casting before it a shimmering sense of enthralled hope, yielded to the chilling belief that cricket had and would become more banal and mundane. It was the year of grace which gave way to the hard years of reality.

8

Pricked Bubbles

Some surmise that cricket builds individual character and establishes its values throughout society. That pseudo-Hegelian claim is without doubt false, for cricket has never actively enjoyed that weight of influence. If anything, the reverse is true, and that is significant enough. The flavours and taints of cricket are shaped and determined by its host society. That is the connection. At any given time, cricket – like any other important cultural element –mirrors and reflects the social frame in which it is played. Thus the cricketing transformation from the careless rapture of 1947 to the hard times of the 1950s, and the longer-term effects beyond, was in chief caused by, and acts as a metaphor for, and the analogous changes taking place at the base of British life. Although all these elements interlock, ease of reference necessitates a simple division, and, at the hazard of some contrivance, it is possible to summarise them as the four Ps: the physical; the populist; the political; and the psychological.

First, the physical fabric of first-class cricket was heir to the same misfortunes as the nation at large. The outward signs of economic faults which had been freezingly exhibited during the winter months of 1947 hinted of a deep-seated malaise. Britain faced a huge post-war debt, and faced it with the sudden loss of American aid. There were continuing, even increased, shortages of raw materials and foodstuffs. Between the third and fourth Tests of 1947, for instance, there was havoc and panic as a run on sterling abruptly deepened the financial crisis. There were bleak austerities, and rationing of some goods continued until the mid-1950s. Despite the gradual uplift in living standards – by 1947 wages were about 30 per cent above 1938 levels: one good reason why many people were able to attend cricket matches – there were underlying economic ills.

From the 'Work or Want' rallying cry of the late 1940s to the financial anxieties of the early 1990s, Britain remained in serious trouble as the country found it difficult to generate wealth and sustain productivity, especially apropos its share in world trading. Inflation was the critical domestic symptom of this disease, although by the 1980s mass unemployment, cured by the war and avoided by the Butskellite consensus for decades afterwards, added its grim presence.

It was inflation which adversely affected cricket. The cosy view was that a cricketing county could exist on an income of £10,000 annually; and that, according to Sir Home Gordon, was too much. There were even thoughts that, in the late 1940s, cricketers' wages might be reduced from their pre-war levels, with a top rate of about £400. The huge crowds led to the complacent acceptance of a grand illusion. The cricket authorities were too ready to believe that all was well, and that their refusal to reform the structure of cricket had been justified. Thus everything was static. Wages were not increased; subscriptions were not raised; and yet, insidiously, inflation crept higher. The post-war socio-economic changes meant that, on the one hand, there were fewer amateurs who could afford to play, and on the other hand wage levels elsewhere resulted in professional cricketers no longer being among the elite of their class. Mediocrity was the outcome.

First-class cricket was badly managed in this era, and several counties verged on bankruptcy. In some despair the financial crisis was solved by the combine of sponsorship, much of it connected to one-day cricket, and broadcasting and allied fees, mostly the proceeds of unending international cricket. Now a county will take perhaps only an eighth each of its income in subscriptions or gate money. Wages are considerably higher, and rightly so, although the top players, in particular the stars drawn from overseas, obviously outstrip their junior colleagues by some margin. By most judgements, including statistical assessment, the cricket is poorer in quality and, if one compares over rates, customers get less value for money.

To turn to our second element, from the end of the 1940s the relation between populism and leisure radically altered. That immediate post-war period marked, in fact, the closing phase of the golden age of collective leisure. Leisure-seekers became increasingly individualised in scope. It was, from the cricketing viewpoint, partly to do with the rise in support for other pastimes, old and new, and the encroachment of football into the hitherto sacrosanct summer season. But it was much more to do with the eventual ubiquity of the motor-car, liberated by the end of petrol rationing. Public transport and public leisure had walked hand in hand, and the decline of one was instrumental in the decline of the other. The car allowed many choices, not least family-oriented ones – the striking incidence of eating out is an instance – and the regular compacting of huge crowds into arenas decreased. Of course, some sporting and other events still commanded massive crowds but, as the spectacular downward spiral in football attendances illustrated, it was no longer commonplace for many thousands to watch an 'ordinary' game.

A major aspect of this was the so-called miniaturisation of society, of which the use of the car rather than the bus was itself an example. Just as the laundry became the washing machine and the ice storage plants the refrigerator, so did the concert-hall become the music centre and the theatre and cinema the television. Stay-at-home leisure has become most pronounced, and, needless to say, television offers an inexhaustible diet of sport on its comprehensive menu. These are no open-and-shut cases: minority attachment to many sports and pastimes is constant. However, between about 1870 and 1950 it was the common lot of man (that gender is used advisedly) to leave the house for leisure and to enjoy much of it in congregation. The era which was introduced by the Great Exhibition of 1851, attracting unprecedented crowds to the Crystal Palace, ended with the Festival of Britain of 1951.

Cricket was a main victim of this change. So little rated did cricket quickly become that the Chancellor of the Exchequer removed the Entertainment Tax from cricket in 1953 – a material and perhaps a figurative comment on the condition of the first-class game. And there was an added gloss. In a more secular and sceptical time, its aura almost of religiosity stood it in no good stead, and, more broadly, its contemplative and complex nature was out of keeping with a faster-moving electronic age. Its temperate virtues had still retained the respect of the sober working class, as well as the middle classes, between the wars. The Second World War had bred, as wartime sometimes does, a more serious cultural complexion, of which the intensified interest in classical music – the army's Southern Command had thirty chamber groups in rehearsal at one time, as well as a full-scale symphony orchestra – is but one example. This middlebrow appeal, this desire for an element of gravity in entertainment which made the Brains Trust a radio triumph, admirably suited cricket.

As a more materialist and consumerist and perhaps trivial approach was espoused, and something like a suspicion grew in many quarters of an interest that demanded a degree of thought and application, so did cricket suffer. An overdose of one-day cricket was, ultimately, cricket's somewhat desperate answer to its crisis of support.

Third, Britain was broken as a world power by the Second World War, and very soon that was reflected in its cricketing politics as well. It had been, on both fronts, a noble effort. Like Nelson at Trafalgar or Wolfe at Quebec, the nation had, internationally speaking, succumbed at the moment of its finest glory. The exhausting endeavour to withstand, for some time alone, the threat of totalitarian domination was fatal, and in real terms Britain was never to be measured again as of world stature, as she had been in the 19th century. Alongside that development, there was the loss of the Empire, which, in some regions, Britain handled more sensitively than its European neighbours with the same problems. Subservience to the USA on the one side, and then the gradual suction of the United Kingdom into the grey anonymity of the European community, completed the process.

Britain has still not come to terms with that basic geopolitical overhaul. The nation, and more particularly its politicians, have never quite managed to realign their actions and rhetoric to these circumstances. It is sometimes said that we have been unable to find a new identity: what has possibly been more damaging has been our inability to cast off the old one. The expectation of greatness, instead of a relaxed accommodation to the moderate delights of ordinariness, has wasted much energy. For its part, the English cricket establishment found it hard to understand that its authority could not be taken for granted, either at home or abroad. The sanctity of cricket could no longer be assumed: cricket had to fight for its place in what sun there was, and had to look hard to its commercial laurels. Abroad, the cricketing nations, alongside their general sporting improvement, expected a little more responsibility. Neither in playing nor administrative terms could English cricket presume even to be *primus inter pares*.

A similar levelling-out affected county cricket, as the generality of funding and the use of overseas players evened up the county competitions considerably. But, just as it might be difficult for Yorkshire to comprehend a nation where they are not top county, it has been arduous for English cricket to understand a world where it is not top country, or at least sharing that honour only with the Australians. The débâcle of the Packer affair, especially in regard of the legal rights of the paid cricketer, was a sharp lesson in this respect. Again, it was a lesson being learned, with similar mental blockages, by other sports, such as all codes of football and athletics.

Fourthly, *vis-à-vis* the psychology or culture of Britain during these times, that sense of ambivalence was frequently revealed. There was an air of disengagement or misplacement. Suez showed a nation reeling between the arrogant and the anxious. Literature, drama and the popular culture evidenced this uncertaintly. The anti-heroism of Lucky Jim; Jimmy Porter's angry tirades; Tony Hancock, buffoon masquerading as braggart – these were characteristic personifications of the 1950s. The integrated culture of the war years overlapped into the post-war period for some years, and although, of course, there were nasty exceptions, people remained 'tolerant, patient and generous'.

The agreed social amalgam, which was parleyed over and fashioned after the war, continued for many years. It combined public controls over the economy and communal resources with some dedication to social and welfare needs. However, from the early 1950s, the mood grew steadily uneasier, and frictions became more apparent. The gap opened between public good and private aggrandisement, and at last the 1980s ushered in a decade of more rampant self-centredness, with all manner of ugly excrescences from football hooliganism and filthy urban environs to gross iniquities and social injustices. Cricket, ostensibly the epitome of urbane value, reflected this deterioration in national ethics and behaviour. 'Pressure' was the shorthand explanation or excuse for poor performance and disappointing attitudes. Big money and extensive media attention created, we are told, the pressure.

Cricket, needless to say, has never been the delectable and pure activity that some of its hagiographers would claim. It has always been competitive, charged with emotions, and subject to the machinations of the cashbox. This is no misty backward gaze through rose-coloured spectacles to a legendary past. There was much that was wrong with both society and cricket in 1947: for example, both were class-ridden and guilty of feudal management practices. Nonetheless, when sufficient has been allowed for the prejudices of nostalgia, it is difficult, perhaps impossible, to argue that the quality of first-class cricket forty years on is pleasanter than in 1947. Quality is utilised in two ways: to refer to the standard of cricket and its capacity to entertain; and to the ambience of the game, and the mode in which players – and crowds – conduct themselves. The word 'pleasanter' is a deliberate choice, for it reminds that cricket is, after all, a diversion, a subject for decent enjoyment.

First-class cricket, and the great crowds that watched it, somehow suited the atmosphere of the post-war years, probably because it was a civilised conduit for men and women sharing, in larger degree than now, if not by any means exclusively, more collective values. Similarly, some may agree that the nation *in toto* is not so pleasant a place to live. It may be richer and more suffused with material artefacts (and that is no wicked thing) and it may be more exciting and stimulating. Yet it is more unpleasant.

Could the cricket establishment have taken steps to avert some of these problems? Eventually, of course, cricket was always bound to have been subject to the buffets of overall social and economic change: one cannot deny the overriding influence of society at large. Nonetheless, the authorities might have prepared themselves a little more astutely, instead of casting themselves in the role of the foolish virgins. Nor is this just a matter of wisdom after the event. In the latter years of the Second World War, when reconstruction was all the rage, many other institutions did seek to reform themselves. The war provided some with a splendid opportunity to modernise and expand. The BBC, for example, was transformed from 4,000 employees and 50 hours radio broadcasting a day in 1939 to 115,000 staff and 150 hours radio broadcasting in 1945.

The disappointing aspect is that cricket examined all the possibilities for change – and then decided to do nothing. It was not as if there had been no proposals for revision in the air. It is highly likely that some basic adjustments at the end of the war, when many people were in the mood for change, would have both ensured a more enduring popular support for all first-class cricket and provided a more wholesome protection for the game when the crisis grew. One one-day cup competition; the creation of two or more divisions, with relegation and promotion; the organisation of regional cricket, in part, as a valuable preliminary to Test cricket – a pattern of change such as that, founded entirely on suggestions made at the time, might have preserved the first-class game in a healthier condition. When, *in extremis*, swingeing reforms were forced on cricket, they managed to be both piecemeal and over-elaborate, and, although the financial standing of the game was saved, the game itself deteriorated.

The summer of 1947, flattering to deceive, played a major part in this minor drama. It was so delectable that all were persuaded that the authorities had been right to eschew fundamental alteration. There was nothing at all meretricious about the actual riches of the cricket in 1947, but its very wealth made manifest too sanguine a promise for the future. No one could dare challenge the golden testimony of that season, and claim that much was ill in the world of first-class cricket.

Once more, cricket thus reflected and exemplified the national mood. The hope that it would continue brightly, kindled by the light of 1947, was of a piece with that general post-war aspiration that a better world would be formed. It was a quieter and less brazenly confident air than after the First World War, but that idealism was still present in decent abundance. Neville Cardus assuredly caught the mood: he was 'deeply touched' in 'this heavenly summer' to observe 'a pale-faced crowd, existing on rations, the rocket bomb still in the ears of most folk . . . this worn, dowdy crowd watching Compton . . . each stroke a flick of delight, a propulsion of happy, sane, healthy life. There was no rationing in a Compton innings'.

Yet by the early 1950s, and after the energetic and occasionally visionary efforts of the Attlee administration had tired, one grew aware that it had been something of a false dawn. The cricket season of 1947 had been, in the words of John Arlott, 'a kind of cloud cuckoo land', and perhaps that was a fair metaphor for the nation at large. However, there is no cause for deep depression: cricket, like so much else, did at least survive. Looking back over the 20th century, at the two world wars, the economic crises, the occasional social turmoil, to say nothing of the retrogressive waste and ugliness of the last decade, Kenneth O. Morgan, its distinguished historian, still observes no fundamental change. 'The face of Great Britain,' he writes, 'like Snowdonia or Thomas Hardy's Egdon Heath, might show surprising changes of light or pattern; but the underlying geology remained the same.'

That is very reassuring. Maybe there will be another season's cricket like that of 1947. Perhaps it will be next summer . . .

Index